Contents

I have waited far too long to write this book, but the timing could not be better. There are too many sales trainers out there who have never walked to walk and only talk the talk. Many of these trainers are great speakers and have good intentions. Many are making their money from selling you on their sales courses and not selling a product or service. I know what you are thinking. Not every coach had to play the game to be a great coach. I say this is very rare. You may cite professional athletes and their coaches who never played. What you need to realize is that it is likely that this athlete has practiced for 15-20 years before the coach gained the player. So saying your sales coach does not need to have played the game, is to say you have been practicing sales skills for years and your coach will build on your existing talents. This is rare but possible.

This may be the case for a few of us. Those of us who ran lemonade stands or competed in elementary school to win the big prize in the fundraiser. If this is you, then your sales coach and trainer can help shape and build you regardless of their origins. I just feel passionate about where you get your information. Their ideas and opinions could give you the wrong idea and expectation so much that you never try something like door-to-door sales.

I recall in 2012 at what was what I would consider being the bottom of the market crash. Although it started in late 2008, it was not until 2012 that I hit rock bottom. I felt helpless and out of options for how to get myself out of this mess I call a career in real estate. I had kept my head above water by doing hundreds if not thousands of broker price opinions for the banks at $60 a task. I would get the orders and drive out to the homes to take photos while my wife stayed at home doing the computer work. I am sure we hold a record for most BPO's done by 2 people somewhere. It was miserable. It was depressing. Remember that scene in Pursuit of Happiness with Will Smith? The bathroom floor scene. How about the one with Dustin Hoffman in Kramer vs. Kramer where he needs the job? That is where I was.

I knew that picking up the phones was a great way to generate business, but it was too slow. It was too easy to ignore the closing signs, and I was just not feeling that the energy I had on the phones.

I was calling 100 people a day, but it was not enough. I knew the only way to get my business back was to take massive action. Physical sweat and effort. It was that day that I printed out a few fliers of recent comparable sales and took to the very first door.

Nobody was home.

The second door. A man opened the door with no shirt on and holding a poodle. It was kind of creepy, but I asked. "Hi, my name is James with Century 21, and I was wondering if you had any interest in selling your house?"

"As a matter of fact I am." He replied. "But you need to talk to my wife."
I asked, "Is she home?" He replied, "No, but we are upside down and we will lose it."

This was very common at the time and by this point, I was hundreds deep in sales experience of short sales. So, I replied, "I would recommend we set a time to meet, all three of us, to talk about the possibility of a short sale."

That was it. I walked off with that appointment and that was the beginning of the beginning of my new birth of real estate. I knocked for over 5 hours a day and started getting paychecks. I paid off the loans both personal and bank. Now, whenever I feel like I am not doing enough to achieve my financial goals in this business, I go out and start knocking. After thousands of times my knuckles have hit the wood and my fingertips touched cracked plastic doorbells, I feel I have something to teach.

These words result from thousands of hours and dozens of blisters. All this time I not only walked and knocked myself to the top, but I also did a lot of over-analyzing of every facet of this technique. After going over the final draft of the book, I would have never imagined I could write a book this big on the topic. I would name it the door knocking bible but then it would tempt me to make religious analogies and throw in some commandments and a few thee and thous to boot. We are in a very interesting time for the sales world and its ability and an inability to communicate with the potential customer or lead. Whether you generate your business from the internet and have implemented technology into your follow up or you are a traditional salesperson who receives leads from past clients, a sphere of influence, print ad or outbound lead generation this book should help you.

Chapter One
Before You Knock

My background in sales began at the age of 7 when I would try the lemonade stand in front of the house and then deploying a few wagons to go up and down the block with a mobile lemonade stand when we had to. It's not like I had an empire, it was more like me, my younger sister and my best friend across the street. We called ourselves the Cardboard People Lemonade. We got this name because we would dress in cardboard and sing a song as we walk down the street. I only remember the chorus line.

By the age of 9, I had taken on a paper route with my bike. I covered about a square mile and I recall the early mornings and toppling weight of the bike on the heavier Wednesday coupon days and the 2 necessary trips on Sunday's paper.

This evolved into having to solicit for new business by going door to door. I cannot imagine that in the 5th grade I was in the back of a covered pickup truck, with no seat-belts, traveling with a group of boys on the freeway. I recall the bigger boys would laugh because they could spit out of the back open panel and the spit would fly out and, in a vortex, fly back in at the younger kids.

Even harder to believe is that we got dropped off in 2's and 3's depending on the size of the territory into apartment complexes to knock on doors soliciting strangers to sign up for the newspaper. I recall there was a clipboard and a script. It was simple. "Hi, my Name is Jimi with the Orange County Register and I am here today to asked if you are getting the paper?" If they were not, I would have to sell and if they were, I would try to upgrade from the only Sunday crowd to the daily. This would never happen today.

Fast forward 2 years into the 7th grade and my family moved to a new territory, and I took on a new route. At a certain age, they gave you the task of handling the money and even worse was collections, cancellations, customer service, and complaints. I recall several times trying to hold a 100-pound pedal-powered Huffy cargo with one hand and throw a 7-pound paper up a staircase in the rain. Only to have it explode in mid-air and scatter in the wind. That meant one paper short and a return trip before my 8 a.m. cutoff.

In high school, I was limited on time and summer was my only freedom. I would go door to door looking for homes who needed their windows washed. Along with leaving my fliers on porches and windshields in parking lots, I did this for a few summers. This was until a friend I hired to help me stole some collectible coins from a home and that burned me out of wanting to expand into larger territories. I was still young and until then; I limited my sales to what I was in control of.

Just before I graduated high school, actually the last semester, my parents moved the whole family to Peru. Yeah, Peru. I was still a kid, and I had a bit of fun but down there, but it only took me a few months to realize there were only two options in that country, either be an actor or a politician. Neither of those interested me.

After about a year, I returned to the United States and joined the Army. Not only did I join the Army, but it was the infantry, possibly the lowest and hardest starting point. There are you get to sleep in the ground when it's wet and shoot lots of guns all day long, but again this was not a path of greatness, at least not for me.

This was honorable, but not the path I wanted to pursue, I got my honorable discharge and I remember the day that I was going through processing to leave. I thought to myself if I could apply just 10% of the effort that I had to exert as a soldier into anything else in my future, I would be highly successful. But what would that be?

I came back to Southern California and lived with my parents for a short time, and that same time, I went to college. I did not know why or what I would do there, I just knew I should be there, so I showed up. It was a junior college, and on the day that I sat down with the counselor they had asked me what I wanted to do, I did not understand. As I scrolled down the list of options. Theater and acting were one option, and I figured that could be fun until I "figure it out." It didn't take very long to believe myself an actor and to be from Southern California I got on a few movie sets but nothing more than just an extra.

It wasn't long before I met a girl whose father insisted I give up acting and take the career path of real estate like my parents. That was the last thing on my mind, but I wanted that girl. So, I hung up my thespian hat and studied for my real estate course. And just like I said in the military, by exerting myself I began a 26 year and counting career as a top producing real estate agent. And how did I generate my business? Purely cold calling. Absolutely no past clients, No marketing, no branding, no sphere of influence. Just pick up the phone every day and making 100 calls a day minimum.

The one advantage I had in real estate was my father was a hard-working buyer's agent and my mother handled the listing of properties and marketing for their successful real estate team. It was just the two of them and then at one point 4 of my siblings came on. None of them remained for more than a few years, I was the only one who took it to the limit. I hate to throw them under the bus, but the one thing mom and dad provided me was a level of integrity and honesty. When it came to sales skills, the only thing I had from them was a large library of Anthony Robbins, Zig Ziglar, and Tom Hopkins on cassette. For those of you who haven't heard of these individuals, they are leaders in self-improvement and sales.

The tactics I learned and deployed were one of the few two methods known in the sales world. I know these methods as active and passive. These two are the only things you need to know about understanding the systems you can deploy for lead generation, client conversion and sales. In the following chapters, I will cover the mindset of the consumer along with the mindset of the salesperson. These are both based on the expectations of both individuals and the timing of the consumer's call to action. Once you have the right mindset and the right expectations, you can better handle the roller coaster of emotions and income inevitable in our profession.

Door knocking is by far one of the most effective methods for generating immediate business and filling your funnel for future business. It also allows you an opportunity to meet neighbors in your territory and get to know the neighborhood and architecture.

One of the most important things to remember is to remember. Remember, every home and every door as you build a knowledge base of the streets and schools. The most important thing you can possess to compete with your competition is knowledge. Not just knowledge of the residents and area but a more intimate knowing of the individual homes themselves. Having such knowledge gives you confidence when speaking to homeowners in the area you wish to one day dominate.

In sales we are limited by 2 elements of nature. Time and space. Not to get too meta, I want to help you understand your limitation to understand your potential.

Time. How much time can you spend in preparing, prospecting and presenting. The 3 P's. There will be several factors that play into your day to day routine. Preparing the material, the software and getting dressed and driving to the locating. These take time. They are all in the preparing phase of the routines for success.

My theory is this. If you want to crush it in the sales industry, there will be levels of effort exhausted in the beginning of your career until you have momentum in a marketplace. So, if this is your first day in sales you will work a lot more hours than if it was your second decade. However, that you consume my content tells me that whether you are a rookie or a veteran, you are not where you want to be in this business.

This book comes from the perspective of the real estate industry as I have been doing this nearly 30 years as of the writing of this book. I also realize that there are plenty of other industries who will benefit from my knowledge of door-to-door sales so I make every effort to be general in what I sell but know that often I am referring to homes but can honestly be substituted for widgets. I tried to answer the questions I asked myself over hundreds of hours at the door. I tried to answer the questions people asked me when they found out I was training others to go out and knock on doors. I often feel like I was always over thinking the act of door knocking but not so much that analysis paralyzed me.

Selling is a contact sport, it is a numbers game, and the name of the game is closing.
The arena you play the game in is your database.-Me

Many of you will find this book will hold the secrets to success only limited by your stamina and optimism. For others, this book will contain the lessons you seek to enter a business that you find scary or unfamiliar but know deep down inside you should try it. Either way, you will find that I have put a lot of thought at the doors to come up with some of these methods and this is very import for you to know. You are learning from someone who has knocked a ton of doors. I am reluctant to say more than a hundred thousand because it seems unrealistic but then again over a 3 decade career in real estate sales this might be true. That you are learning from someone who has overcome a fear or reluctance of knocking on a complete strangers door to becoming a successful salesperson should inspire you.

Things do not come easy to me. I don't get lucky. I have found out the hard way that either I am doing something wrong or everyone is lying about their success or at least not telling the whole truth.

The more contacts you make, the most opportunities you will have to fail. The more you fail, the more chances you will have at figuring out how to succeed. If you put in the time to generate a database of people who need your product or service, and you follow up effectively with them, you will sell.

In my experience, I had to put out a tremendous amount of effort when compared to what the "gurus" would suggest. So in this book you will find numbers that would make your head spin and your feet hurt just thinking about it. This is a good thing.

Although I am perceived as a hard closer and an aggressive salesperson with a "beast mode lead gen" attitude and a push, push, push system, you will find out I am just the opposite. It is because I do not push the customer into a contract or harass a buyer to "close the deal" that I rely heavily on what I call the "law of probability."

The more people I can come in contact and follow up with, the better my odds are. But because I am not a "hard sell" guy I have work harder to put myself in the right place at the right time and build relationships with people who say, "maybe." That when they say *"maybe one day,"* today, I place them into a database that reminds me to call or email or mail or send valuable information over days or years to build value to my brand. That one day when they place the order they will think of me because I was not pushy, but I was persistent and consistent.

Therefore, I say I am not lucky. It is why I believe that if I can do this, so can you. Having the right expectations before you knock, and having the right words when you do, and then implementing effective systems for after you walk away, this is how you will overcome your fear and convert more sales. Avoiding being a pushy door-to-door salesperson and instead having a belief in your product and a pride in your work that demands you find everyone you can to help before they end up in your competitions hands, who you know will not appreciate the job and cannot possibly care more for the customer and the outcome than you do.

Just open your mind to the possibility that there is an easier way, the old-fashioned way, belly to belly, and be more productive and proud of what you do.

Many of us salespeople will want to know every little detail of the product. Prospecting to generate sales can be difficult if the consumer shows an interest and we stall or stumble in fear or excitement. I recommend you use prepared scripts and dialogs at first until you develop your own style. Forget that it may feel canned or prepared. Most sales industries have a handful of objections that a consumer can give. If you prepare with just those you are good to go. If your company does not have a script, then you must build one that gets the customer's attention as fast as possible with a follow-up plan for the next call if you do not make the sale or set an appointment on the first call.

Having too many mentors for something as specific as door-to-door sales will also lead to confusion. If you are the kind of person who enters YouTube for hours at a time looking for the secret sauce or an easy way, you may be hurting yourself. Often your reluctance to head out will be from a lack of confidence so you want to be ready. But this is not like tennis or weightlifting where you can warm up first. I cannot stress enough the value of grabbing my few and simple lines and get out there. If you ask 10 "gurus" about what to say and how to say it you will get 10 answers.

Worse than spending your valuable prospecting time on learning past the basics is to learn from someone who has never been to the door. It would surprise you how a good deal of water cooler trainers there are. These individuals have taken every course on the subject and we may know them for their training. I am not impressed by someone who teaches about weight loss if they were never fat. Meaning that you should really make sure that the person who is teaching you how to sell has sold more than just their products to teach you how to sell.

We sometimes need role play partners to do a dry run over the objections that may come up during the knock. Having someone read lines like an actor could help you clear the jitters and fears of beginning the sales process. I still recommend that if you have a large database of potential customers in a community that you just get out and fail forward. The lessons you will learn on the first few screw ups will be the best lessons you will ever learn. Preparing to knock on a door or preparing to make the first pitch will never train you as much as failing at the first door will.

I suggest that you make the sale in person as fast as possible with the least amount of knowledge. Trial by fire and learn by immersion. If you are on a car lot selling automobiles, I would strongly recommend you walk the lot without the customer and learn the brochure with all the specs. To this day, I print the documents and specs on the properties and just go. When a customer asks about a year built or days on the market, I look at the specs sheet. If there is an answer, that I cannot give I use this simple script. "I *don't know but I can find out.*" Then I deflect away from my ignorance on to something that I know about.

If you just signed on with the company and it is your first day, there is absolutely no shame in admitting ignorance with the scripts in one hand and the company manual in the other. If you have the personality and are a pleasure to work with, the customer will be more than glad to put up with your lack of knowledge in the product. Nobody ever has the sales process memorized in the first hour so put in the work and put in the study time. If you want to be great, then put in the overtime too. If you insist on learning everything about the sale, then I suggest you do it after hours. If you have to learn everything about your product, then depending on the variety of factors apply, you may get away with the summary, where some industries you may need to know what you are talking about.

Chapter Two
Mindset and Expectations

You don't want to "HAVE TO" but you have to "WANT TO." - Me

The two biggest reasons agents avoid the doors are either they are afraid or they feel that is beneath them. Maybe some think it does not work, but those are the ones who have never tried it. And by try I mean knocking on 100 doors and asking one question. Do you have any interest in selling this house? Don't knock it till you try it. People at the door are mostly very nice. You will seldom run into a bad apple. Do not let that bother you. I promise that if you just keep walking, you will get results. The quality of leads you will generate in a very short time for very little money is worth it. Maybe physically it is not possible. Then you are not likely to even be reading this. I cannot speak for those who suffer with real pain and the physical limitations trying this method of prospecting.

Even though I have run 7 marathons, 26.2 miles, and consider myself to be athletic-ish, I too have my limits. You might not even consider that to knock would hurt, but it does. Knocking for several hours is the equivalent to running several miles according to my body and my step tracker. For others it may be more or less. This, like any other workout, needs to be tracked for improvement. Start with a watch and see how long you can go. Then try to beat that time the next round. Trust me when I say that the first time will hurt. The second time may hurt more if it's the next day. However, there will come a time around the 5th-10th session where the hotspots on your foot, chafing on your areas, nipple rash or soreness diminishes. You will build a door to door knock callous and it will get easier.

Different from fear is a reluctance to go out and knock. It is usually something that you do when you are satisfied or complacent and have nothing driving you. You lose your vision for why you're doing it and you don't do it.

Complacency is more likely the culprit. If you do not "have to" sell to make this month's payment then you won't. Are you willing to do whatever it takes to succeed? Prove it. You have no one else to answer to but yourself. If you are expecting to increase your results at the doors than you should know better than to assume this will not happen without action. You have to do the work to have an expectation. Maybe you thought this would be fun and easy. The fun is what others show on the internet, but they never share the pain. Complacency is the favorite of all sales people's excuses they just don't call it that. It manifests itself in the way of fidgeting at your desk, cleaning out your drawers, taking an early lunch, and having multiple bathroom trips when you don't really need to. Leaving your phone on, and your door open and making everyone aware that you are available for idle chatter are several ways that reluctance appears.

How do you overcome knock reluctance? You have to have a "why."

A purpose and a damn good reason why being reluctant is a terrible idea. What if your significant other was watching you right now? Would you be in trouble? How about your boss or your kids? Can you handle stealing time from either of them to stare aimlessly at the screen or sky while they think you are working hard? Guilt is a great motivator.

Another tip for overcoming reluctance is to schedule your day and stick to it. This seems like an easy decision, but are you aware of your time? If you become reluctant and you check your calendar and the block of time allotted for now reads "doors," then doors it is. If you have scheduled a lunch, then it's lunchtime. If you have the discipline to time the time during your daily preparation, then you should build the desire to stick to it.

As I write this section, I am afraid to check my schedule because I am sure I am out of time to write for the day. I can check this on my watch or on my phone, and I am constantly reminded of what I should be doing. After many years I have developed a sense of responsibility and obligation to do my work. I have set goals in the beginning of the day such as 100 doors. If I know that I take 3 hours to knock on 100 doors and it is 3 hours before sunset, I cannot just sit. My problem is that I will sit in my car for a few minutes until 3 hours before sunset because I like the pressure of having to rush. I know it's the opposite of productive but I am human.

The repetitious boredom of mundane actions, such as hitting the doors, is like some people who work hard at the discipline of staying super fit. Bodybuilders work in the gym and you can see it. The greatest athletes in the world face reluctance. Just watch interviews online. Their ability to break through the reluctance is the difference between them and the other players. Make a goal to never be reluctant for more than a few seconds. The hesitation is reluctance and the repeating of this hesitation is often referred to as delay. Don't delay.

Either you are or you are not a Salesperson. No mother has given birth to a salesperson. Never has anyone been diagnosed with salespersonsons, I made that word up. Yet, something sets apart the greats from the average and from those who really suck. The funny thing is that there no template for knowing who will succeed. It is only obvious when you see what's in their heart become action. Their desire and passion blended with discipline and tenacity. I see the spectrum of salespeople from the top to the bottom and to this day I can not figure out how they succeed. I believe I am an introvert and an extrovert. If you put me in my element, such as the zoo or an amusement park or pretty much any vacation, I am fine with putting myself out there. I will talk to anyone and make eye contact with complete strangers. If I see someone sitting alone I will chat it up.

How can I even suggest I am in introvert when I hold a camera all day long and share my life on the internet? Easy. I use it to keep myself on the edge of discomfort to get out of my shell. I did recently read, or audio read, a book about introversion where there really is no such a thing. Because the element and environment make the inclusion and involvement. Sales have nothing to do with introvert or extrovert. It is an effort. My father used to say *success is a mindset*. I say it is a mindset in action. If you have some reluctance to picking up the phone or knocking on the door, it is all in your head. How do we get out of your head, whatever is in there? I go to the worst-case scenario. Believe it or not, the worst-case scenario is actually not getting business from these efforts. But no one ever really thinks this is the one to fear. The one feared most is the "*what if they are mean*?"

Have you ever met a mean person? Did you die? Probably not. What happened? I am guessing it frazzled or rattled you for a few hours. Nobody likes confrontation. The reality is though that the confrontation did not last. You went through it and then it passed. Maybe it took a day, maybe it took an hour. There was a time when these "confrontations" would impact me deeply. I would shudder at the fear of an individual having the nerve to "threaten me" or "come and get me." They never did.

I really want to write a profound statement about overcoming fear, but I cannot. I have no fear. I am not afraid to knock on a door. Why? Because if I do not knock on a door, I will have to get another job. I cannot afford to pay the amounts of ad money necessary to keep a roof over my head while I wait for business. I have heard fear is False Evidence Appearing Real and perhaps this is also true.

Overcoming fear in other parts of my life are addressed by knowing that if the worst-case scenario happened, I can play it out in my head and overcome it. Most of the time we fear the unknown, but that is like being afraid of ghosts. I suppose I am afraid of ghosts. Does this mean I won't sleep in the dark? No. I am only afraid of ghosts when I see them and guess what? I have not seen them.

Let's play with this though. This "worst-case scenario." One that I deal with often. What if a dog runs out and attacks me? That is a reasonable possibility. In my mind I have prepared an outcome. Here is that play. I walk up to the door and I knock on a screen door that is flimsy and slightly open. I see the resident is across the home and they see me. But not one second later their big vicious Pit Bull Rottweiler Doberman Hybrid with horns and red eyes flies at the screen and breaks through. I take a few jumps back and hold out my forearm and feed it to the dog. I drag it out to the street onto public property and if the owner or the dog has not remedied the attack, I will do my best to defend myself. I talk a big talk now, but when wrestling my dogs in fun I have never thought about the offense, only the defense. Obviously if it is not a police dog there is the likelihood that it will not just grab an arm and not let go but that it will continue to attack more than just the arm for a criminal take down. I sure hope that this planned confession does not come back to bite me in the butt... literally. I have no intention of being mauled for gain or confirmation or profit. I know that should this happen there will be both physical and emotional damage. Lawsuits may happen and medical bills will arrive.

There is the worst-case scenario for me. Besides the dog killing you. In that case you are dead so it will not matter. Lets be real though. It will not happen. You cannot use fear as an excuse not to work.

Yes, it is possible to become immune to rejection. You can only take so much of the same punishment over and over before you go numb. It's not that you become immune to the rejection, but more that you begin to accept the realization that this is a process necessary to achieve acceptance. If everybody said *yes*, well, I don't even know what that would mean.

There are several methods for training and conditioning your mind to overcome fear. I don't believe that there should be a fear in sales. To be afraid would mean that you are in some physical danger. There is no physical danger in prospecting by door. Unless you ran into a crazy occupant or a dog.

Is it really a fear? Or is it a reluctance or is it the uncertainty of the unknown?

I believe it's just from the uncertainty of the unknown. So let's address what we know since everything you could face I have probably been through. At the door there will be people who try to insult you, and maybe even scream at you. Actually, I've had nobody scream at me at the door, well maybe one but I think he was medicated. And that was after 50,000 doors. However, on the phones, it is very common for people to insult you because there is nothing for them to lose by using foul language. I've been doing this for so long that hearing somebody use those words on the phone surprises me and energizes me in some weird sadistic way. I'm always amazed someone would speak to somebody over the phone like this not knowing anything about me.

Is it really rejection? Is somebody taking you as a person and summing you up and judging you as being worthless and rejecting you from now until the end of time? Is it really that extreme? I just don't believe that anybody can reject me, I don't let them. To me, true rejection is somebody looking at you after years of hard work and telling you you're useless in the workplace. Maybe that's rejection. Rolling over in the middle of the night and asking your significant other for a little something, something, and having them say *no*, now that's rejection.

20

A complete stranger telling you they're not interested in what you have to say is not rejection, it is actually them not being interested in what you have to say. It's the equivalent of asking them if they would like a free tattoo of a butterfly and them telling you no. Unless they are in fact interested in getting a tattoo. It's not that they're rejecting you as a tattoo artist but that they are not interested in a butterfly tattoo. We can reduce this rejection to the ridiculous. Problem solved

Perhaps this will help. If you knew how many people would have to tell you they're not interested in order for you to achieve your sales goal, that might set you up for the right expectation. It's like running the distance of a marathon. If you knew ahead of time that the marathon was 26.2 miles, you would not feel as if it was the end of the world if you trained properly to do 26.2 miles at mile 17.

In the same sense, if you knew that it took 1000 attempts at a sale to achieve your first closing, you would not see it as an obstacle but as a path. In a marathon, you follow the path; you take the steps and you will ultimately end at a finish line. With no rejection and absolutely no fear of the unknown. I believe the worst thing that could happen is that you never get a sale it all. Even this would not be a matter of failure, but more of not knowing what the target is. If it took you 5,000 doors to get a *yes*, and you got upset at 3,000 doors, that would not be very realistic now would it?

No, you should not have any fear. Worst-case scenario, I say have a few drinks before you prospect.

Let's face it. The door knock is the same thing as the cold call. Therefore, my script is quick and simple. Many times, the homeowner will stand there puzzled at how easy it was for them to get rid of me. Sometimes, residents are disgusted with your existence and you would be more welcome as a flaming paper bag filled with dog poop. The best thing to do is smile and thank them and walk away. Therefore, it is so important to track the doors with notes or an app so you never go to that door again. Every once in a long, long while you will get someone who makes threats, says what you are doing is illegal or might even yell at you or insult you. Again say thank you and walk away. Mark the door as "do not knock." Honestly, I prefer to know that the individual is a jerk right up front then to find out later. It will save me time in the long run. Besides, do you really want to deal with difficult people? Crazy I can handle, but difficult is tough.

Let me tell you two stories and how I dealt with furious people so you can hear some worse case scenarios and maybe you will learn something that will help you get over your fears.

I was door knocking in the middle of the day. The first door I hit was a great lead. Which later turned out to go with an agent they had. Oh well. The second door nobody was home. The third door was a nice lady. As I walked to the fourth door a man about 5 and a half feet tall and about 150 pounds and about 45-years-old began walking up the street towards me. He was yelling, asking if I just knocked on his door. I said,"yes I did." Then he asked if this was my car. I had parked it right in front of his home, by coincidence. I said," yes it is." He then screamed, "Get this F'ing piece of Shot out of here!" as he threw my notepad that I left at his door. As I was walking up he was ranting and raving like a madman. Either he was on medication or just coming off. Either way, I had never had someone so wild as he. As I walked up to the car, he was trying to set me off. Lucky for him I am a pacifist. Otherwise, there would have been blood. As I got into my car to move it I saw that he motioned to my hood as if he spit on it. I got out of my car and looked at the hood and saw no saliva. "You got a problem?" he asked. "No problem," I replied as I got in my car. He was still screaming at my window and I had to poke the bear a bit. I rolled down my window and asked," What happened to you in life that makes you such an angry person?" He just kept screaming. This one kept me off the streets for the rest of that day. I overcame. I am over it. The following day, I asked a neighbor across the street, if that guy is the neighborhood crazy person and he said yes. Also the fact that I parked in front of his home when that street is parking by permit only because of the school nearby. Moral of the story? I should not have parked there. He should have a no soliciting sign if he hates door-to-door interruptions. He ended up selling a year later. I knocked on the door recently. No one was home.

Another time I was knocking at a door and a man opened the door only to have his dog run right out. He walked past me as he went to get his dog. The dog kept running as I stood there like a jerk. The man turned to me and said, "If my dog gets hit by a car I will sue you." I just stood there wondering if I could help. Luckily the dog came back. I got about 2 doors before he came out again and yelled. "Hey!" I thought to myself, "Here we go." He walked up and said he was sorry and that the dog means a lot to him and that I should not bother people that way. I explained that as sorry as I am this is very hard work but to achieve success in this business I have to do the hard stuff. Outcome of the story? He became a friend and now when I know I will knock that area I bring a bone for Radar, that is the dog's name. This happens to me about once a month. The dog running part. It is very awkward when the seller says, "Oh don't worry they will return." As I walk away to knock on the next door and see them still chasing the dog.

Avoiding doors that read no solicitors and keeping your script short and sweet seems to work very well. Most people are quick to get rid of you because they are used to door-to-door salespeople being pushy. Often I confuse the homeowner when I say thank you very much have a nice day and walk away. It's like " prepared them to be harassed for another few minutes. I believe giving them back their time is the best thing you can do. Be confident, be fast, be courteous and be gone as soon as you know they are not interested.

One time I had someone call me with troll like aggression asking me if I left "this" in their driveway. I engaged them in a conversation with pleasantries and answered his interrogation with honesty. He was insulting about how there must be a better way than to litter. I then explained to him I know it's not common but I do not want to spend thousands of dollars on advertising only to get no results. That he was actually lucky that most agents are not willing to work this hard to find customers otherwise he would get more of this. That I did not get to meet them and only left it hoping to get a call. In a sad story tone like pity me I have to work to feed my kids. It turned out he was interested in getting an estimate on his home. I set the appointment that day. He and his wife turned out to be the coolest people ever. Him and his wife actually told lots of jokes. NO kidding like knock knock type jokes. He is an Army vet and turns out he knows a lot of high officials in the city and is even in charge of the weekly flag ceremonies and veteran events in the community. A pillar of the community and loved by many. Being that I am a veteran we hit it off and I attend the Thursday flag ceremony often and a few other vet events and we hang out at them and talk real estate. As of this writing, I don't have the contract but each time I am in a crowd with him he makes a point of saying if you need a great real estate agent this is James Festini.

Now that I think about it, I had another one like this but not so productive. A man came out of the home and asked if sales were that slow and desperate that I would go bothering people at their homes. I told him I was sorry to bother him and that there are only two ways to get business in real estate. I either spend thousands of dollars on the internet and pray to get contact or I go out the old-fashioned way. Sure it is hard and there is a lot of rejection but when you have to feed a family and want to earn an honest living in sales sometimes you have to go through this. That again I was sorry. He changed his tune from being a jerk to and seeing that he did not know this was the way and that he was not interested and to come by anytime. It always blows my wife away how I can diffuse human bombs and I also believe this is my superpower. I believe it is by being honest and passive. Pleasant conversation always diffuses confrontation if you know exactly what to say to make the person feel bad about being mean without triggering a full on atomic annihilation on your preferred prospecting method. I share a few scripts to overcome resistance in my chapters on what to say.

You need to determine how many doors you need to hit to expect results. You MUST give it at least a month of every day doors. Although I cannot speak for everyone, I can speak for me and my history. I have a door knocked in 3 different counties and it works. The key is speed. Make sure that if you are not "feeling it" that you go faster. You must knock with a consistent pace and rhythm so you never feel it "not working." I can feel like a failure in this business at times but the time I overcome the impossible is when I knock fast. If I am knocking slowly, I feel the failure more than ever.

This door knocking is emotionally exhausting. You are putting yourself in the most intense series of rejections that one can have. People will say no to you and they will look at you when they say it. Don't take it personally. Some people will even insult you by slamming the door or giving you a look that could kill. Some may even yell. There is something about teenage males that keep happening. I am not sure why, but I seem to get the testosterone throttled a-holes that have no respect and they show it. So, what? I just think to myself that they will probably live as a-holes that have wives that can't cook or clean and their kids will be a-holes to him one day. Find your humor in the rejection. Find your tipping point for success.

Mine is 100 doors. I have never gone 100 doors without an interaction that makes me want to knock more to get more. My system is for those who work like a beast but have the strength to work through doubt.

If it is not working, maybe you are not listening carefully enough. If you have ever walked away from an interaction wondering if that was a *maybe* it probably was. If you have ever walked away from an interaction and wondered if I have asked one extra question, you probably had a lead. I have been at the door and had this happen. I get it, this is scary sometimes. It happens to me too, even after hundreds of thousands of doors. You got to be ready to ask for what you want.

You must know your numbers to know if you can ask yourself if it is not working. Sure there are days where you will knock on 100 doors and have no results. Then the next day you land 5 in a row. There is no rhyme or reason that I can think of for this phenomenon. Sometimes there are neighborhoods that hit more than others. Then again, those same neighborhoods that I have gained dozens of leads have yet to pay off. Even though I have a half a dozen people who keep saying next season James. Next season never comes.

Your following through is just as important as the follow up. If you do not prospect you got nothing and if you don't follow through you get nothing. Perhaps if you are comfortable enough, you could ask the follow up even if they don't hint at deserving it. Asking each time," Do you think maybe later?" and see if they trigger your spider senses. There will be days that you will feel you have knocked on 100 doors and you are burning out. Therefore, I recommend you track your effort along with having a goal of 100 or more. If you look at this and see you are only at 50 and feel like 100, then maybe you need to rethink you perception. Whatever you do, you cannot give up.

I promise you, if you hit enough doors using these techniques, and read this book more than once you will pop one off, and that will give you hope. There will come a time when you will land such a good lead that you don't just walk away, you float away. This will be one where they let you inside and give you all their information and tell you exactly what you want to hear and you will say exactly what they wanted to hear and you will set an appointment and you will be closing them that week. Man, I get pumped up to go now just typing this. I have had these where from nothing I am getting a $15,000 paycheck 30 days later! Sure, it's rare. But it is also possible. My floating experience happens about every 4,000 doors. Find your floating experience tipping point and aim for that. Keep your eye on the prize. This works. If you work. This does not mean nothing happens for 4,000 doors. You will still get leads for follow up.

This may be the hardest part about being a one-on-one coach. I will have students sign up and after 20 days I can sense it frustrates them they are not getting the results they expected. I expected that they knock on 500 doors a week minimum. And they did not. How can you measure results with no effort? Don't fool yourself. If you are not being held accountable by someone like me, you are the only one that you can lie to and believe that lie. It is not working because you are not working. Sales is a numbers game. It is a contact sport. And the name of the game is lead generation and the rules are follow up. Play harder.

Chapter Three
Preparing to Knock

There are only two ways to acquire a customer. They either come to you or you go out and find them.-Me

There are only two ways to acquire a customer. They either come to you or you go out and find them. We can call these passive and active methods.

When you advertise a property or a product for sale, whether online or in a print ad in the newspaper, the expectation is that the customer will call or inquire about your goods. This is where a skilled individual with the right scripts and dialogs can capture that inbound inquiry, convert it to a lead, and hopefully get the sale. Many companies have yet to realize that just getting an inbound call is amazing, but that's not the end of the sale. It is critical at this point that the vendor has systems in place to convert the inquiry and if that does not happen in the first contact that there be an effective method for communication or follow-up until they are ready to buy. I outline these methods in this book.

I consider it passive because the vendor, or salesperson, spends time and or money to expose and advertise their product, only to wait for the customer to call in. Although this is an effective method for gaining customers, there is no clear-cut path to success. There have been millions of hours and dollars wasted on placing the wrong ad or setting up the wrong website only to be ineffective at generating inquiries.

Especially in the real estate business and many other local businesses that rely on recognition and reputation. Once you become a well-known business in town, the clients are more likely to call on your service. Most times it is not even the specific ad that goes out but the constant branding efforts over the years that had them remember you. But until then it is a gamble. I say local marketing is like an engagement for marriage with a commitment to maintain a consistent drip campaign. Sending out one mail piece just won't cut it.

I recommend a plan with mailings once or twice a month for the first year and then once a month forever. Yeah, forever. You don't see Coca-Cola backing off, why should you? Now I am referring to a local business wanting to market through traditional print products. Whether someone delivers your pamphlets at doorsteps or you negotiated to be on top of the local pizza boxes or even mailing postcards. Not necessarily location-based ads like billboards, but more of an outbound brochure left at doorsteps or on car windshields in a parking lot. Clean marketing pieces with a unique selling proposition and a call to action. This is expensive and there is a lot of trial and error but still works to this day. For the salespeople who do not have time to wait or money to spend, this is not an option. This leads us to my area of expertise.

Active marketing. This exists on two platforms and no other. I like to say this as a bold statement because many can argue there are more but I have put a ton of thought into this. The two active methods for "active" marketing are face to face and phones. That's it. This book will dive deep into one of the most effective methods for active marketing and show you what it takes to get the customer to say, *maybe*. Then if you do a good job of following up, you will be there for the *yes*.

There are more than the five avenues of marketing but only five approaches to connect with a potential customer. These are the five levels of communication. They are the five levels of lead generation. They are the five levels of follow up. These are the five levels of the funnel strategies broken down for today's consumer and sales force entities.

The five and only five are:
1. Print. Mail and Posters or billboards Kiosks and booths.
2. On screen. From TV to banners and ads online including those on social media.
3. Digital. Email, Text, SMS, MMS, and DM or Direct message.
4. Phone calls.
5. Doors. Face to Face.

No more, no less. Of course, you can say word of mouth but many of these *lead* to word of mouth and I am sure you can track every sale on earth to these 5. The goal is to get to a place in your business where word of mouth is over 80% of your income. This is the holy grail of all those who seek to grow from a sales position to taking orders from customers that line up out the door.

The first three are passive and the last two are active. That's right. If you mail, email, stand in a booth or even send a direct message are you not then forced to wait for the customer to respond? Only when you engage in real time, can you actively communicate with the potential customer and not be left hanging and waiting for an answer to your question. Word of mouth is also passive but again it is likely you earned word of mouth through one of these five in the first days of your business growth.

The interesting part about these five levels of follow up is that they are also in the reverse order of effectiveness and cost effectiveness. I often refer to the salesperson as the marketer, and the consumer as the market, the lead, the prospect, the suspect, potential customer, recipient or even inquiry, just to make it easy for any industry to understand the process of customer acquisition.

A store front in the right location could survive and even thrive on foot traffic alone, but at some point, they will want to expand or at least keep a customer base for repeat and referral business. But now we are talking about the local restaurant whose owners have been in town for 3 generations. You can't tell me that there have not been their share of difficulties that a salesperson or a marketing campaign could not have helped. If not, then they are the exception to the rule. It is likely they survived on word of mouth and location but a few bad reviews in this, a review economy, and they will suffer a loss. Then to keep new faces coming in they must implement one of the other five methods.

This business of sales, and this book on selling, is focused on startups and those who want to grow. I am speaking to the small business and to the large corporations trying to understand the evolution of communication in a "swipe left" society. In a world where people find convenience by touching a finger on a piece of glass in their hand. Here you are desperately trying to get new business and your competition spends just enough money on ads to get that lead. Luckily for you, you know where they live and as long as you move fast enough you can catch them before they click the screen or make the call to your competition. Your presence will solidify a face to a name and if you hit it off and follow up, it costs you nothing.

Interestingly enough, the five levels of marketing also appear to decrease in cost to the salesperson for lead generation and customer acquisition. With print ads being the most expensive and doors being free. I know, in many cases, you would argue that you are buying time by spending money on ads, but that money you spend is probably coming from time you spent earning it. The risk of spending money on the wrong platform for hoping and waiting a return on investment could be costly if you don't crack the code fast enough. There are so many clever marketers selling you on how to get quality leads using online ads, radio, TV or print ads. They will share results from other customers and their case is very compelling. The crazy part is that in the real estate industry, if you looked one or two levels deeper into their claims you might find out the individual was not an agent and cannot point to a real result.

I will often see blatant lies to generate their own leads into their funnel to sell you on the same thing they are using to sell you. The problem is that *your* target market is not that easily fooled. In the real estate industry, like no other, I see so many bright-eyed suckers looking for the magic potion or the easy button. The marketers are getting very good at capturing them too. One time, I saw an ad in a new real estate agent feed promising to grow their Instagram followers by the thousands. The ad claimed that they grew one account to over a million followers. This was a claim that I had to investigate. It turned out he was on the team that helped the country of Cuba grow to over a million followers. Crazy, right? I don't think Cuba needed the help and I do not believe that a single salesperson will cross over one million. Not unless they are a celebrity or the face of a brand that is a celebrity. This is such a scam, and it drives me crazy.

The First 3 methods are so much easier to do. Just spend money on someones sales pitch on how easily you will close deals and repeat. I believe this is probably why my content and system remains so unpopular. Although I use the first three methods in my practice, I am not a big fan of sitting around and waiting for the results. They may never come and I would be out of work. If you are going to spend money to advertise, make sure you don't sit around and wait. Go out and hit the doors.

When I started my sales career, I was primarily doing outbound telephone prospecting. There was no door to door until after the crash of 2007, nearly 15 years after I was already established as a six-figure producer. At that time I was using the telephone and a headset. It wasn't until 2012 that I took massive action for my business and its' growth and recovery from the market crash. On the first day of knocking on doors I generated a lead that I got under contract within days and the rest is history.

I prefer the doors over the phones. Why? Because the secret to my success the first time I made 500k in real estate was in a market that all I did was cold call until I got an appointment. This has changed. The doors give me better leads and more of them. The incubation period and turnover of lead to contract seems to be almost the same but the amount of leads I get in an hour on the phones and the quality of these leads are way better at the door. People cannot hang up on you at the door. People are nice. If they are not, I mark it in my app and avoid them next time. You see there will only be one limitation on the number of doors you can knock and that will be on your physical tenacity.

There is no best time to door knock, only worst times to door knock -Me

I have knocked tens of thousands of doors. During these sessions of door-to-door efforts, I have kept notes and stats so I could increase my results. One day I went out and asked myself this same question. What is the best time to door knock? I headed out at 9 a.m. and went the entire day. I hit about 400 doors by the end of the day. Actually, I gave up 2 hours before sunset because I landed a fantastic lead and set an appointment for that same day. I listed it too. She ended up being a total nut job whose dog I was deathly afraid of. She ultimately canceled in the beginning of an escrow and nearly got sued by the buyer for breech of contract. I think she still lives there 10 years later. Oh well, you can have her I have already cut my losses.

The result was that I could see that regardless of the time of the day; I got 24% of the doors to hear my script. I did not count the individuals who were renters or non-decision makers, so for those of you outside of real estate, your odds may be better to reach people who do not need to be a homeowners to be a prospect. The renters and non-decision makers were about 2%, the ones that had a no soliciting sign were about 4%, and that leaves the ones that did not answer to about 70%.

I found that the people home during the day seemed to be nicer though. Perhaps maybe because they may be retired or not working. On the flip side, I also notice that after 3 p.m. I would get a few more kids, and after 5 p.m. I would hit what I call the A-Hole hour. What is the A-Hole hour? I have found that of my decades of outbound sales there seems to be a time of day that without even looking at the clock I am suddenly catching the rudest people. They seem to be those who are responding after 5 p.m. I have a theory that they are usually just home from work and would rather not hear about my whatever and are likely handling dinner or family matters and don't care to deal with any salespeople. Even if they were thinking of selling their home, I was probably not there at the right time. My other logic is that most telemarketers believe that the best time to call is after 5 p.m. because more people are home, which is less true in this day and age with mobile phones and active lives.

My suggestion is that you can door knock from 9 a.m. to sunset or 8 p.m. whichever comes earlier. I feel that going to a door before 9 is early even though some areas are legally OK with 7 a.m. to 9 p.m. I say good luck with those times. There are homes for example, that have long corridors with overhangs that when you get to about 15 minutes before sunset the entryway is dark and feels late. I am not at all comfortable going up to a door after the street lights are on and sometimes when I can see the photosensitive light come on as I walk up. If you can see the lights on in the house, it may be too dark. I know that there are people who do not have any problem with this. I suspect that knocking in the winter at 5 p.m. when it's already dark will decrease the number of doors that will open regardless if it's only 5 o'clock. I think if you are trying to knock at night, it's because you were screwing around all day and now you feel guilty. Try again tomorrow.

Even though I never really set out to measure on purpose again, I never stopped knocking. After so many doors I can still say that the 24% open rate works just the same on most days. I have never knocked on a Sunday just because I try not to work that day, but I usually do open house. I have seen Friday nights to be good and for some strange reason Thursday nights feel slower. But that does not mean you should not knock. You can use that excuse because I am not using it.

Oh, and for those of you who ask, what about going back later to those who did not answer? I have tried this and found it to be a total waste of time. Knocking on doors that do not answer for sure is a sure way to increase your chances of knocking on doors that do not answer for sure. However, if you are in an industry where your territory is quarantined or protected and you are limited, or maybe like in real estate you want to establish your farm by knowing everyone in a small community, then mix it up. For me there were always plenty of doors that would get me my 24% open rate and let me feel productive rather than frustrated. So the best time to door knock is not after sunset and not before 9 a.m. every day but a holiday that you know is not good to be at the door.

Let's use my typical day as a template for what could be your day.
Below is my schedule.

Summer Schedule
8 a.m. Be in the office preparing the day.
9 a.m. Follow up calls by phone then knock doors.
1 p.m. Lunch
2-5 p.m. Telephone follow up or doors
5-8 p.m. Door knock with telephone follow up on hot leads.

Winter Schedule
8 a.m. Be in the office preparing the day.
9 a.m. Door knock for 3-5 hours.
1 p.m. Lunch
2 p.m. Door knock
5-8 p.m. Phone Prospecting with telephone follow up on hot leads.

If the thought of you working on prospecting for 6-9 hours makes you cringe, you may not be cut out for such a routine. However, you will need to find an effective method for generating leads. I know there are only 2 ways to get business. By finding it or it finds you. If you are not known enough then you will have to spend a lot of money on being found or time on finding the prospects. My methods come from a place of aggressive lead generating. Gathering so many leads early in the game that the time will come where you are only doing follow up on high quality prospects. Focusing on those that I find and those that contact me from my initial contact and effective follow up.

I have always used a list of information for tracking during my door-to-door efforts. For my industry, we are in a position to market to a select group of individuals based on geographic areas. This is what we call a farm or territory. In a specific territory, regardless of your industry, you will want to track the data for re-purposing it. In some cases it may provide current and future value to know the occupants status. Like if the home is vacant or if it is rented. Maybe the property is a multi-unit or a single family dwelling. It helps to know if they have a no soliciting sign in the yard or a for sale sign in the yard. In the past I was slowed down by the data and found out that most of the time the only data I wanted was to have the address to log information into.

Nowadays there are a few applications that you can carry on your smart phone when you go door to door. I will not be mentioning any of these in the book because these apps have evolved for the better and some for the worse. My favorite at one time, the one I used for about 7 years, launched a new version and began to phase out the old. The new version was better suited for larger companies and industries like solar panel sales and pest companies. Many of the features I got used to were moved or removed and it made me look for another option. When I first discovered them years ago, they were one of two in the app store. Now there are dozens and maybe hundreds. I will only go over the features and benefits that I found to be useful and compare to explain how I settled on one.

The reasons for using an app instead of paper or memory are many. There are a few that should convince you to use one today. Let's say you are walking down one side of the street and mark those not home and those who are home. Then as you are going back on the other side of the street, you see a homeowner pull into the driveway or they are now standing outside watering their lawn and you marked them as not home earlier. You look at your app and you can see that they were not there before and now you can go back across and approach to hit an owner that you would have missed. I suppose that if you could remember every door, then this would not be awesome.

Another scenario is that if they have a no soliciting sign and you mark it. But then on the double back you spot them outside. You can approach them at the street, and they don't know that you know about their sign. So, you can approach them without being concerned about their sign that you cannot see from the street. Let's say you download the physical stats like if they have a pool or equity for pool companies and solar sales. This would be valuable to know what kind of potential is behind that door. There are many list providers that will give you several other fields and data sets to target. In real estate, I leave no door behind. After hitting the same neighborhood two times a year, I am familiar with the homes that have nasty owners and no soliciting. I also have on my app those who were nice and even those who I am in communication with.

The downside of these applications is that you end up having two databases. Technically, two CRM systems where you are tracking results and follow up. My solution to this has been to use the app during the day and then go back to the computer at night and log in only those who were leads. The rest of them do not matter. One extra step I have to take is to indicate with some flag or status on those leads that I know they have been processed and moved into my real CRM. The one where I follow up by phone and email.

One of the most important features of these apps is the ability to track you using GPS. However, if your signal is not so great some apps get laggy. One app had the ability to fence off a parameter of 500 or fewer homes, than it would gather recent sales data of these properties. It would have photos and statuses such as sold or for sale, bedrooms, baths and more. The problems I had with these apps is that I love to draw on maps, the builders and tract codes, and some developments were over 500 homes. This app also made me pay attention to what side of the street I was on and each time I crossed and turned on a new street I was standing there playing with my phone. That is the last thing you want to do while you are out knocking is waste time playing on your phone. Every second counts and every step and movement adds up.

Another great function of those that use GPS is the ability to see yourself walking to the door. You can spot a view or if they have two units. With the mapping features you can see large lots and streets to plan a better route. Starting on one end of the street and crossing and going back to your start. Like the postman, you must be efficient and strategic in how you walk from the beginning to where you will end. They call this *"park and loop."* The postman told me also that streets with only one side with homes is a *"dead head."* These guys are the masters of door-to-door efficiency. I am currently using an application that as I walk up to the door, it pulls up the address without me having to tap on the roof on the map as the dot moves. The only downside is that if I forget to tap on the previous home and complete a disposition like lead or not home, I physically have to step back and near the missed home and wait for the GPS to render. There is an option to seek the address, but that is a pain.

There are also apps that you can get for free from title companies. I have not tried them at all. I used to value being able to load data from my CRM and have it in my hand, but there was so much information. Especially if you load a bunch of data from a list provider. I am going to the door with my agenda. If you see my script, none of the words I use have anything to do with what I know about them. In fact, I think it's creepy to knock on a door and address them by name and know how big the home is, etc. If you come up to my door and I don't know you and you say my name, your either a religion stalking me or a paid assassin. OK, maybe something less dramatic, but I still dislike it. It does not help the situation. Even If I knew the back story like an expired or for sale by owner, I would still open with my intro and question first. I must break through that 8 seconds. If they are receptive I can say, *"wait a second, wasn't this place....?"*

Test out every app you can and find one that works best for you. I am sure if you go to my website you might find the one I recommend. Just know that the information you have at your fingertips is there for efficiency and not to slow you down. It is a place to track your results and to measure your effort. So many times I have gone out and felt like I did 100 doors only to see on the app I was at 70. If you like to challenge yourself to 100 a day, then having this on an app is great.

41

The greatest advantage of using your smart phone at the door is as a part of your presentation. When I am at the door, whether I am carrying a messenger bag with notepads or a pocket full of cards, I usually have my hands free to allow body language to flow freely. Except for the one thing they are familiar with, the phone. Small, sleek and simple, I approach the door and hold it close. I walk up to the door and I tap on the screen and cue up the contact card on the screen. As I am communicating and I identify them as a lead, I am flawless in my delivery of that awesome script. *"Would it be OK if I could send you out some information on the market, I can email you, it's no problem, what's a good email?"* I then look down at the phone and do not look up until they say it. This body language is common and friendly in today's world and it works most of the time. Then the cherry on top is when I play the Columbo redirect and tension break into idle chatter just after getting that info and as an afterthought I say, *"sorry, what's your number?, 714…"* as I look down at the phone and wait for them to complete the next 7 digits. That is a total sales Ninja move to get the number almost every time. See my scripts section on how to balance these physical actions with the right words and then my chapter on body language to incorporate your body.

Individual results may vary. Individual effort will verify.-Me

Most people want to know what is the ROI or return on investment of door knocking. To answer that question with a blanket response would lead one to the wrong answer. Sure it may encourage you or discourage you based on an expectation. For example, some may think they should get a lead for every 50 doors knocked and that the lead can be under contract that day. The reality may be that you get a lead but maybe one that it not going to sign a contract for 6 months.

I can tell you *my* results. With a disclaimer. Individual results may vary and individual effort will verify. Every agent and every market will be different. Several factors will apply. If there is a low turnover and there are very few sales, this may cause fewer closings. If you are using my script wrong or any script the wrong way, this will also land you in a place with less success. If you dress like a punk, a slut or a hobo, and sound like a fool or a crook you may not get very far. You are making dozens if not hundreds of first impressions and maybe even presentations. Every moment and movement matters. Every mumble or mess up will take a toll on the results. That said, I get 3-5 leads for every 100 doors. Out of 100 leads I will get a listing lead that will sign a contract within 3 months but maybe not with me, there is still that to contend with. I have also noticed a strange fact. That for every 4,000 +o- doors, I will find a person who is ready to sign a contract within seven days of that meeting. Now, do the math, and do your own study.

I have heard some sales trainers say you get a listing for every 25 doors. To this I say, tell me where this is and I will knock on 300 doors a day and own that town in a month.

After 90 days of 100 doors a day, you can have around 100+ names in a database. As you generate leads you are also raising and lowering the status of these leads from hot and ready to close to cold and just a suspect who felt better at the door but was not really a lead. Not throwing them out but also not considering them as a potential paycheck in the next year or two. That means within 90 days you could build a database of names that *nobody* has. Sure some of those individuals are in databases that have phone numbers. Many of them will already have an agent and most of them are garbage.

Wait… what? My leads are garbage? Yes, all of your leads suck. The odds of you getting a listing from a database of 100 self generated leads is low. There is a strange thing that happens when you speak to someone in person and they say they are interested. They change their mind. They forget you ever existed. Worse than that, they never respond or answer their calls. I call this the disappearing lead phenomenon or being "ghosted," and it's real. This does not mean it is a waste of time. Far from that. The leads travel through three degrees of motivation. They begin as a nothing, a cold call or door. Then they are a suspect or inquiry. Then they become a prospect or a lead worthy of following up.

That is why the Internet lead is such a difficult process to convert. The "lead providers" refer to their inquiry as a lead. When they are only a step above a name in the phone book with a curiosity for what you might be selling. Qualification become the most important aspect of following up on these individuals. Consider the funnel strategy. The funnel strategy is a theory that if you stuff as many names and numbers into a funnel that only a few will come out of the bottom of that funnel as we filter them based on their readiness to transact.

Now you are at a door and an individual says that they "might" be interested. This individual could be 1 month to 3 years out from having a need. It is up to you to take the *maybe* and put a future day on it. By asking qualifying questions you can determine an approximate time to not only follow-up but to expect them to make that decision.

There will be instances when you will be at a door and the homeowner says that they are in fact thinking of selling and they already have an agent. The next few words will make or break the individual into two columns. *"Maybe you can close them"* or *"you never had a chance."* You ask probing questions about time lines and pricing to deflect from the close so they open up to you. Should they mention the name of a specific agent or a relationship, then the odds are that you are out. If you ask if they have interviewed agents and they say *no*, chances are it was already predetermined who they will hire. The relationship is too solid for you to break in. But knowing that you almost had one and feeling a tug on the line and it got away, should be enough proof of concept that prospecting by door works. Don't be discouraged. Be encouraged and inspired to move faster. It is behind the next door that you knock that could be your next paycheck. You have to do the work and get good at your craft and always adjust your expectations for each area and as you get better at this you will close more sales.

***I am a human pop up ad that makes it easy to click the "X"
without accidentally opening the ad- Me***

I often hear people stating that they want to go to the door and
provide something of value. I feel unless you are offering free car
washes or to pick up dog poop for free, you have no value. Your
value is in giving them back that which you took... their time. Even
in the real estate industry I hear people saying things like we "just
sold" or "just listed" a home and let me tell you about it and then ask
you about your plans and won't you take my recipe and note pad
please. Come on man, this is the worst of all offenders in this day
and age. People can get this information online if they are interested
and your note pad is killing trees, especially when it goes straight to
the can, assuming they even accept your lovely gift of garbage. OK
fine, maybe that little old lady who loves notepads and recipes wants
it, but you know it is going to the hoarded pile with every other
agent in town who leaves notepads. I do notepads. I just do not do it
this way.

The reason the door is better than the telephone is that enthusiasm
can work face to face. On the phone I do not believe it does. Well, at
least not for my industry and maybe most. I know this flies in the
face of every book and lecture on telephone sales but ask yourself
this question. If I call you today and you see my caller ID and do not
recognize it yet you reluctantly answer. Then I jump through the
phone with enthusiasm and say your name like as if we are best buds
and I have great news, what do you think? I immediately know you
don't know me and you are selling me something. I am skeptical and
cynical and as a telemarketer of sorts for over nearly three decades
this approach is an immediate hang up. Before caller ID it was easier
to get away with this approach but now people answer the phone
pre-judging you. Especially as of this writing telemarketing, robo-
calls, and spoofing along with phone scams, we are a society of
reluctant phone conversations and many prefer to text over talk.
Why am I talking about calls? Because of the five levels of
marketing, door knocking is probably the last active marketing
avenue left. Forever and into forever. Never to be another method to
demand results now versus spray and pray with passive outbound
pay per click and print ads. Door to door sales is the final frontier for

a salesperson to go out and sell. The other methods are for marketers.

As salespeople we are being forced to evolve into marketers that create sales copy and spend time and money trying to push ourselves in front of consumers hoping that they fall for our "call to action." The difference between door-to-door sales and every other marketing or sales tactics is the difference between right here right now and RSVP. At the door, delivered just right, to an interested or even slightly interested person, you can ask for the business and get the answer. Every other method besides the phones you have to request on their terms and schedule. If someone more assertive approaches or even pops up on a screen just at the right time, they will win the sale. It is getting harder every day to put yourself at the right place and time when that place and time is in their pocket, while on the toilet or in bed. By this I mean on their smart phone.

I believe that I am a human postcard, I am a human side banner ad, and I am in their *"actual"* feed and not their digital feed to be ignored. I am a human pop-up ad. The difference is that instead of one of those pop-up ads that the "X" to close out of the screen is smaller than your fingertip and you accidentally tap it and open the ad and get mad. I make my "X" large and red and I work on my images and presentation to capture your attention and if you are interested, you click and if you are not you do not. I feel that most salespeople are the worst offenders of this pop up analogy. They are that pop-up ad that makes you watch the first 15 seconds of the video before you can skip or close. You know what I mean.

I believe that we are interruption marketers and we are traditional sales people too. This combination makes us very disliked by the public. Nobody enjoys being interrupted. So how do we avoid this impression? First, we have to understand why we are despised and what is it about our actions that make them mad. Is it we are saying something that offends them? Is it because they are not interested in our goods or services? Nope. It is because we are robbing them of the most valuable commodity that all of us have but not in abundance. Time. We are wasting their time. We are keeping them from whatever they were doing before we showed up. Now you arrive and because you are enthusiastic about your whatever they don't want, you are trying to shove it down their throat.

Have you ever had someone like this knock at your door? They are very nice and often fantastic at their delivery. They are very skilled at their pitch and somehow their script does not have any perfect moment to tell them go away. So you just sit there until they are done trying to build rapport and be a buddy. I get it, some industries this is the only option. For most industries however it is unnecessary. This long drawn out monologue before you even know if they are a prospect could be shortened and refined to just a few keywords. Again, a contact is a person who "can" say yes but maybe they don't. In other words, a qualified decision maker. I believe that with a well written script and a short and sweet delivery you should be able to pitch and move much faster, thus giving the prospect back their precious time sooner. If they are interested, they will show it. You may have to look hard to see it but over time you will develop this intuition.

There are many moments that I when I walk up to a door and I deliver my script, and it stuns the prospect that when they say *"no,"* I am quick to thank them and leave. They sometimes will ask, *"that's it?"* If they do, it is because they are so used to being subjected to a long disruption and my approach is light and refreshing. However, if they do say, *"that's it?"* I will ask the follow up with, *"Well, are you thinking of selling later down the road?"* to which they say no and I proceed, *"Then that's it, thank you and have a nice day."* Being courteous of their time is the best gift you can give next to a smile. Respecting their time by giving it back as fast as possible is the only way you can feel good about doing this door-to-door thing and provide value.

There is a better way. This book is the better way. Just get in and out, give people the least painful experience at the door and walk away. When it's over and you will be better off.

Gaining trust in less than 3 seconds will be easier if you look trustworthy -Me

Professional workout gear is what I call it. What do I wear? I go for 3-6 hours at a time so I prepare for this as if I prepare for a long run or a hike. The shoes are the most critical part of your outfit. I went to the Walking Store and bought a pair of dress shoes. No sneakers! You don't think I would love to wear my Chuck Taylor high tops because they are cool? Remember, we are trying to cover a wide demographic and have dozens of mini presentations to do. You would not wear sneakers to a listing appointment, would you? If the answer is yes, then... wear whatever. Anyhow, get a pair of loafers or dress shoes that are designed for walking. Ladies, same goes for you. I know it's harder but I am sure there are walking/dress shoes. I think it's weird to see ladies in those orthopedic shoes you see 90-year-old rocking at the nursing homes. You only need one pair as you will wear them over and over. No one will notice.

Your feet will be the first body part to feel the pain. The right socks are the key to survival. I say that if you are wearing loose fitting shoes, and it's a hot day, then dress socks may slip and slide in the shoe. So wear wool socks or whatever is not cotton. Cotton is just terrible. In the military, we wore wool socks, and at first I thought this would hurt and sweat. It was only sweat, but as for blisters, there were none. When your shoes are a bit loose, then you may need thicker socks to stabilize the movement in the shoes. Should your feet move around in the shoe too much, you will end up with a hot spot that turns into a blister. When I wear cotton socks, I need to wear them in a shoe that is tighter. For the times I wear dress socks, I wear them in a tighter shoe. Each person has a preference. I like my shoes snug. You just have to play with it. The wrong shoes or socks will have you laid out the next day or even days if you get a nasty blister. I find that wearing dress socks or wool reduces friction and potential for blisters. I own a pair of dress shoes I bought from The Walking Store and one I bought from Cole Haan with Nike soles. They are super comfortable. Make sure you carry shoe polish in the car for those last-minute touch ups before you go knock.

What you wear is very important to your door-knock success. Finding the right combination of comfort and professional attire is easy for men, not so much for women. I am just guessing, but as a man you can get away with wearing the same outfit 5 days in a row and not be a big deal. Not the same for women, unless you are going to different areas each day. If you knock every day in the hot sun, I have prepared a few hints that you will find to be useful. If it is in the winter, I would recommend a full suit, in the summer I would say a polo with slacks. I know you want to be cool and stylish but what you don't realize is that you never get a second chance to make a first impression. When you door knock you are required to look great, sound great and command respect in a very short time. The more professional you dress, the faster you will give the impression that you are a pro. Think of this. You are doing multiple presentations I guarantee you are making an impression. Gaining trust in less than 3 seconds will be easier if you look trustworthy over hip. Same goes for the ladies.

I bought a Nike "golf" shirt for about $80 online that is both cool in temperature and moisture wicking. Be careful not to get whites or grays cause you will sweat and it will show unless it is a moisture wicking style that has a slight sheen so that even sopping wet you cannot tell if it's wet. Also, if you wear the shirt 5 days in a row, it may show salty dry lines. Mine are black and as long as I stay clean and don't sweat the day before I reuse them up to 3 times before washing. I have 5 of them so I am always ready. I also had my company logo embroidered on the breast where a badge would go. A badge is a must but embroidery is better. If you know a local shop who can do your shirts, then do it. It may cost $10-$20 but it's worth it. If you are with a company that the logo is very recognizable this will help in the appearance of trust.

I have found that on hotter days I can soak my black golf shirt, and I mean soak, in cold water, by pouring a cold water bottle on it and wringing it out and wearing it. It does not look wet if you have the right shirt. After a few hours it evaporates, but it sure helps me stay cool. Along with carrying a frozen water bottle that melts just fast enough for me to sip but not so fast that I run out too soon.

I also wear an undershirt to stop sweat embarrassment. Most important is my "Runderwear" or athletic briefs. If you are a runner or an athlete, you know that cotton is terrible for sweat. There are moisture wicking underwear that you could buy to avoid friction and a rash. I buy the Target brand called Power Cool long briefs. Also called performance briefs. This is for both men and women. You will thank me later. No cotton, check the label. You will chafe and bunch like crazy. Play with the fashion until you get it right.

Chapter Four
On the Street

Identify a territory first by asking yourself "How many doors can I knock on in 6 months and how much can I spend as my farm grows?" Weighing the territory is a balance of time, distances and financial thresholds. Although I am not a huge fan of spending thousands of dollars on mailing out to random people, I recommend that if you can afford to manage a steady marketing effort that coincides with your door-to-door efforts you will be that much more effective at getting to be the household name in the area.

What territory in distance can you master with the time you have to invest in this lead generation method? Finding the territory is easy. You take out a map and put a pin on your office location, and a pin on your home. Then overlay the high school, elementary and junior high district boundaries for your personal residence. Hopefully, these will form parameters to keep you from going too far out of what we will call your *sphere of intense interest*. I say the school district because over time you are going to be interacting with members of your community that share a bond. The two most common factors with neighbors are schools and churches. If you have children in the school system or go to the church, your odds increase that you will enter what I call their *sphere of impression* and ultimately what I call your *sphere of recognition*. This is the ultimate referral machine in most businesses. The goal is to be so popular and top of mind for your product or service in an area that people say, *"I see your brand everywhere."* This achievement gets you tons of business.

Some may choose an area with a high turnover or a high possibility of a sale because more residents move more often. Often it is a low end market that will attract first-time buyers or even investors. The problem with areas that have a high rental rate also means that you are likely to have more renters open the door. If you are selling a product that is not related to the subject property like solar or selling the physical home, than this might be great. If you are interested in finding buyers to sell homes to, then it is possible to convert them. I often find though that renters who can buy are rare. Most people who can afford to buy rarely rent. Unless they are expecting to leave the area. Maybe that is just an excuse because I am not a fan of hunting down buyers for homes as much as I want to have sellers of homes to contract with.

You can seek areas with a geographical advantage, such a hillside or body of water to "land lock" your sphere of recognition. I have found that when you have a community that does not spread in every direction, this lends itself to a cornering of the marketing efforts like a gatekeeper. I worked an area for 15 years that was surrounded by empty land and one freeway in and out. This forces communities to frequent the same businesses and schools and keeps you in a popular advantage when you couple your door knocking efforts with other marketing methods like mailers, sponsorships, volunteer opportunities and other very public events.

If you find there is an area that has a very dominant competitor, most would try to avoid that area. I would have agreed years ago. Until I became that dominant agent. Then even if you are popular, some people will not use you because they think you are too busy or heard a rumor about you driving the neighborhoods with a bullhorn shouting marketing propaganda in the streets. Like the ice cream man for real estate. Yeah, I was accused of this once. You can't make this stuff up. There was this one guy who suddenly was out door knocking when nobody was door knocking. I swear he was watching my videos and using my stuff against me. I must have lost 4 listings to this guy in a season of selling. When I finally met him he was the nicest guy that looked like Vinnie Barbarino from Welcome Back, Kotter you know the character that John Travolta played back in the 70s? I am not kidding. I swear the dude walked and talked like him and even down to the big feathered hairstyle; he was likable. He was beating the competition at their own game. I do this now in an area that is dominated by one guy and it works.

You should also know the areas with physical limitations or restrictions like gated communities. Many of them have a sign posted at the gate that says no soliciting. No trespassing signs are a clear sign that you are not to even walk on that land. I am not a lawyer but I have done a bit of homework on laws pertaining to dog attacks on private property and the one strange but true caveat is a closed fence or gate and a no trespassing sign. Some neighborhoods have a high amount of chain-link fences, gates with a courtyard or tons of hills and stairs. There are areas that have very large lots or long driveways. There may be areas that might have lawsuits against builders or high associations or taxes that might make it difficult to sell the home. If you do not have many choices, then you might be forced to adapt. I have a student who lives in the Bronx in New York and I know that they are not allowed to walk up to those buildings and buzz the doors at the top of those stoops. You know like those you see in movies? But he can go just outside the city and there are more than enough doors to knock.

Besides your wardrobe there are several items that I can recommend that you carry with you to make your life easier. There are so many things that I would love to bring with me, but if I am going on a long hike, I would like to only have the necessities. Being that I consider this a workout, I would recommend you figure out what you can carry for long periods of time without chafing or blistering or getting a rash.

I carry with me what some call a messenger bag. This is a black leather briefcase looking item that has a professional appearance and has several pockets along with one large pocket in the middle. I can line up about 100 notepads on a notepad delivery mission. When carrying a bag or side bag you might want to pay attention to the amount of pieces of marketing you pack with you. Perhaps you can also get a feel for how many items fits into a hand or a specific pouch. You can count these ahead of time so that when you head out you will have a goal of unloading the entire contents of your bag. I carry this bag over my shoulder and across my chest. I can reach in conveniently and grab a marketing piece with little effort as I walk up to a door. The motion of the delivery or stealth drop must be like that of an archer reaching into his quiver. Inside of the extra pouches I would carry Chapstick, gum, business cards, my car keys, my wallet, and sometimes a selfie stick.

I used to carry too much water and too many items for the mission. If you walk up with too many items, the residents might pass a judgment too soon and prepare that "no", before you even say anything. Walking up with a clipboard would make you look like you are there to gather information that they probably do not want to share. I have also been asked if I was a cop because I was wearing all black and my logo on the shirt along with a side messenger bag. I also believe that many times people would look through the peephole and only see a silhouette of a large black figure with something menacing on the hip.

I began freezing water bottles on hotter days and as I would walk the water would melt just enough to keep me hydrated. I was also using the ice cold bottle to cool down my phone because when it would overheat it would start turning black and I could not read it.

That was until I noticed a small amount of moisture inside the camera lens and also saw my screen glitching. It took me some time to figure out what was going on until I saw small droplets on the inside of the glass. Condensation was penetrating the otherwise water proof phone. As a side note, I have noticed that my iPhone would go black faster than the Samsung Note phones.

Another hack I would have for hot weather scenarios was to bring a bottle of freezing water and a bowl and fill the bowl with the water. I would then take off my shirt and drench it in the bowl of ice water and squeeze out some moisture and throw it on. This may be harder if you are in a car. I would be careful not to get the waist area wet too so that when I tuck the shirt in, I would not have a wet belt and pants. I know what you are thinking, that I would look like a wet dog. That is not the case. If you find a moisture wicking material like the golf shirts and test it with liquid, you find that some colors, like black do not look wet because they already shine because of the pattern and material. If it's a hot day, the evaporation will keep me cool for at least an hour or two.

I like to listen to audio books and podcasts while I am out on the streets to pass the boredom. This may seem like a lot to do all at once, but once you get the hang of the doors and get in a groove, you find that listening to some great music is a real pick me up. I purchased a small Bluetooth ear-piece on eBay for less than 15 dollars the fits inside of my ear. I am telling you now that your Bluetooth ear-piece is lame, and it will not work. The one I have is very discreet and has a good sound. I picked up two because they were so cheap. Just search for world smallest Bluetooth and see the models I am mentioning, they are shaped like a yin yang half-moon like item. I recommend black, again for simplicity. Do not do beige it will look like a hearing aide. If you get two of them, you can always have one backup.

Before you hit the doors, you will need to create the material to deliver, this is what I refer to as propaganda. Although the term is usually derogatory, I like to consider it a form of valuable trash. Some will glance at it and most will toss it.

To make these pieces at home, I would recommend you get familiar with the Power Point program by Microsoft. I am only saying this because I really enjoy the drag-and-drop ability of this software. There are a few key elements needed on the piece. I recommend that if you want to have an outside company do this, ask them to create a document that is reusable. I often prepare my propaganda in small quantities on my computer. I use special paper which is a 120-pound white card stock. I will take the paper and create a template that is a landscape design. I do this on both sides with a 3 up vertical pattern. This means that I can create 3 marketing pieces from one sheet. Two sided 8 and a half inches tall and 3.67 inches wide. Tall rectangles that can fit in my hand or in my back pocket. Depending on the marketing piece it will either read SOLD or JUST LISTED in big red font on one side and a mini flier on the other side. Otherwise, if I am just knocking on cold doors, I would have one side filled with sales in the immediate area and on the other side a nice photo of me with a logo. I would also include my disclaimer and some info on how to reach me. Simple is most important. I see so many marketing pieces with way too much crap on the page and it gets too busy to read and looks bad. Less is more.

If you can afford to step up your marketing game, I would suggest that you order some notepads, pens and the plastic bags to hold them. I would take my previously mentioned card sheet and stuff it into a baggie with the pen and the notepad. The only problem with this propaganda is the weight and bulk of carrying them. If you stuff a carrier back with the goods, then make sure you have a nice branded carrying bag. I am always thinking of ways to brand those things I carry, and your messenger bag is not a bad place to stamp the company logo. Walking up to the door with a bag gives the impression of a door-to-door encyclopedia salesman, therefore I am selective with my bags. I imagine that the people who open the door are waiting to have me pull out a spray bottle of green liquid and cover a stain to clean it up to sell them a refill. I feel that if I have my card sheets in my back pocket and phone in hand; it gives the impression that I might be a neighbor or someone in the neighborhood. It's not normal for someone to go door to door with so little in their hands. Can you tell I over think this? That's a good thing.

I have also created marketing pieces that have, on one side, been professionally printed to be glossy, UV coating and all that fancy stuff. I will leave the other side blank with no film or text so I can put it through a printer. It is hard to describe the template without showing you but imagine a tri-fold brochure. Now cut that brochure with a paper cutter and now you have three equal pieces. These same pieces also fit perfectly with notepads. I request that the printing company do not cut them. It will save you money and make it easier for your printer to handle the job of sticking it in the tray. That way if you have custom front pieces universal in style with the back left blank you can customize the content on the back. The more quantity you print, the more you will save at the printer. Especially when you nail down a great design and find a good printing company, you will have a nice stack of ready to print propaganda.

I have often broadcast a live stream of my door knocking as I hold my phone in my hand. One question I would always get is why don't I ask them if they know of anybody who is interested. I can often tell if that individual is open to having a conversation or not. If they step outside and engage in a conversation, then I would ask something to that effect. I would not make it a practice of mine because again I am there knowing I am not providing any value only taking theirs in the form of time. If they are pleasant, then I will strike up a chat. Having the marketing pieces in my hand is a conversation piece, but only if they ask, *"What are homes selling for around here?"* This is an obvious engagement in someone open to standing at the door for a minute. Whether they are a lead is something else. Again, if there is a 3-5 minute chat as they wander out to the front and begin pointing up and down the street divulging all the drama of each neighbor, then I will ask. It seldom leads to anything. Even if they do know someone, it is not like they want me to use their name at the door or give me their number. I have to go with *"a little bird told me."* Which I would never use. I would only walk up to the home, pitch, with an expectation, if I listen carefully for the *"no"* that means *"maybe,"* and if I don't hear it I will still hit them with question number 2. *"Do You think maybe later down the road?"* Read the section on the scripts to understand these steps. If you want to ask every person the question, go ahead. I do not.

I also hear salespeople say things about "providing value" at the door and what do to leave. I do not need a "just listed" home in the area or a "just sold" approach. I believe that when you are preparing something to leave at the door, it should not be a part of your script. At least not for real estate. I hear scripts like this.

"HI Mr./Mrs. Name? My name is Agent with company, how are you today? The reason for my visit today is that we have recently listed a home at 123 main street and it is a 3 bedroom home with 2 baths and a large yard. We listed it at $xxx,xxx and We would like to invite you to our open house this weekend and Do you or anyone you know have plans of moving now or in the near future?"

I just cannot see that in the age of technology that a resident would have the time for you to deliver information that they can get online without you interrupting and spitting out over 20 seconds of verbal vomit. Again, if you want to provide value with a marketing piece. Make your time at the door the least annoying unless they are open to hearing you. Even polite people do not want to talk to you, they are just polite. There is a sign I see at some doors that reads, *"Do not ring the doorbell, seriously, don't make it awkward."*

There will be occasions that you will get invited in. Even in this situation you will have to make it quick for the consumer to find value. If you spend a ton of time with someone who is not interested, this is worse. If they seem interested, then you should leave your propaganda or better yet set an appointment.

I know that many of you think you will hand out marketing material. In some industries your marketing material is one item that you take with you everywhere. Perhaps your tri-fold brochure costs so much to reproduce that you leave with a string or a GPS signal to track it in the trash. Just kidding. But your stuff is in the trash within 90 seconds of you handing it off.

The worst logic I have ever seen is an individual who goes door to door and if nobody answers they just leave leaving nothing behind. They walk away from 75 out of 100 doors with absolutely no effect. Therefore, I always recommend that every door receive a piece of literature. If your tri-fold costs too much to leave at every door than carry a cheaper one for the stealth drop and save the good ones for the hand off.

How many times do you think you will engage a prospect long enough to hand them your material? How close do you have to be standing in their personal space to hand it to them? I assume that you are not 10 feet back when you ask them to take your info. I am big on personal space and rapport building by playing a dance of dominance and submission to get the customer feeling safe and trusting. Sticking something in someone's hand after they have said no is nearly impossible. Placing it in their hands before the pitch would place a thumbtack in their hands and make it even harder to read a *"no"* because they are not thinking *"yes"* or **"no"** they are reading and processing information and with a knee jerk response they will always say *"no."*

There is tremendous advantage in the method I call the stealth drop. As you are walking up to the door, you are looking up to identify an ideal placement spot for your propaganda. One where the person who may answer the door will not see, and the marketing piece will not get wet in the rain or from sprinklers or fly away in the wind. Obviously the mailbox is a terrible place if you read this far in the book. Sometimes the stealth drop will vary in placement based on the size and shape of the propaganda. Sometimes I am walking with a notepad inside of a long baggie. This baggie has a 1-inch hole at the top for easy hanging on lots of things from bushes and plants to fence posts. It is also heavy enough that I do not worry about the fly away and it is in a bag so the water issue is solved too. However, this propaganda is very heavy and I prefer to travel light. I have marketing pieces that are an eight and a half by eleven sheet of paper chopped into three like a brochure fold but cut to maximize one page into three pieces. These are light and fast to drop. I also have them hole punched to make it easy to pop onto a rose bush or branch. Sometimes you will see a small garden flag or even the hat of a garden gnome. Wherever I feel is not a terrible place. If there is a memorial to their deity of a dead family member, that would not be cool.

Do not touch the mailbox or step on a lawn. The reason I call it stealth is that I do not want anyone to see me drop it. I want it to fall or land where I want it to go without the occupant seeing this. Ovoid at all costs having this land on the ground. This will appear like lazy littering. If I see an occupant on the other side of the car or across the yard doing the lawn, I will slip it into a place where they do not see me do this. Why am I so weird about leaving my propaganda without being seen? Because I do not want to take it home. How many of you have a pile of propaganda in your car, your office or your home just sitting there. Don't you think it would be more effective on someone else's property instead of yours? I think you need you play hot potato with this material the moment you obtain it. Make a game of it. I have had situations where the stealth drop happens after the rejection. They catch me sooner than I see them and then as they turn their back or shut the door I drop.

The logic and insistence on this happening is this. When you go to the door and deliver your pitch and they say *"no"*, how many touches do you get with your brand? Probably one if you can't hand off your propaganda during a chat. Now, if you walk up to the door but drop your propaganda and then deliver your pitch, then get a *"no"*, how many touches do you get? Two. When the individual walks out later that day or week and they come across your stuff, they may think to themselves that you are working it. I have had no one say, *"hey did you leave this after we talked?"* If they ever said that I would just say *"I don't know."* I know that two touches and brand impressions does not seem like much, but to me it is a 200% improvement. Even if your impression and engagement allowed you to put your propaganda in their hand, how long do you think it will last before it hits the trash can? I have had people walk out after I walk away and see them take my propaganda to the trash can at the curb. No, do not dig it out of the can.

Here are a few variations of the drop. If there is a screen door, do not drop it in the space between the screen and the metal. You know that pocket where they would have to shove their hand to fish it out. Even if you see a few there already do not do it. What's up with occupants that never collect them? On the flip side, I have seen homes that have a basket full of propaganda. Like it is ready to light on fire for warmth. Lay yours on top unless your drop was out more towards the driveway. I am not comfortable having to touch the door handle to distribute my propaganda. I have had people open the door as I am walking up and if I am standing there looking like I am trying the knob, oh man. Talk about scaring the crap out of them and then trying to recover. You got to be real smooth. Like, step back, chuckle and smile, and deliver. If it looks like the object perfect for placement is a valuable treasure like a prized rosebush or the antenna of their classic 57 Chevy do not touch it. If my propaganda is heavy enough, I will flick it under cars as I approach. This is great because they won't find it for days. The placement is ideal if it can be seen on the next day. Separation of brand impression and the appearance that you are working double and not dropping trash.

Hanging it on a kid's bike handle I think is fine as long as the kid is not standing there holding the bike. The Ushnisha, or the crown of hair, is the three dimensional oval at the top of the head of a Buddha statue, would be a bad place along with the top of a cross with Jesus on it. Touching lawn decor with any chance of disrespect or a threat to breaking the item might trigger someone's anger.

If you are a company that leaving your flier is not practical or you are not there for leaving information but to engage and leave, then a drop may not make sense. For example, Girl Scout cookies can make fliers… why not? Solar sales, for sure. Selling magazine subscriptions, maybe. If your industry is one where you could benefit from leaving your material then why not? If you will go through the effort of walking up to every door, then you should double your potential by leaving your calling card.

Now you are out on the streets and you are walking. You may think it is just a matter of walking up to the door and asking a question. Oh no, not at all. There is something I call the approach. You must remain aware of your surroundings as you walk up to a door. I will point out some things that you may not have thought of but by knowing these you will be a better door-to-door salesperson.

Walking up to a door you should know that you are not allowed to place your marketing material on the mailbox. Although you may never get pinched for this, know that I have it on good authority that touching a mailbox is a federal offense and may be equal to tampering with mail. I have had the mailman call me once, when I hired a kid to do my delivery of fliers and I warned them and I guess that I was not clear enough. Luckily for me I was friends with the mailman but he let me off with a warning. You may not be that lucky. I am so cautious that if I see a massive decorative column that houses a mailbox I won't even rest my propaganda on it. Even if it would save time.

Another thing to consider on the approach is that you never walk on the lawn. I once went door knocking with a student of mine and he kept stepping on the lawn. It drove me crazy. Some people are very protective of their lawns, go the long way around. It shows respect. There will be situations were hopping across from one home to another when the driveways are separated by a small wall or a strip of grass, then I am fine with doing this. Again, each approach will be different but you will now have an understanding along with a heightened awareness of these varieties of approaches.

Look around to see if there are no soliciting signs or beware of dogs signs. If you are walking up to a door, you can observe so many items that would give you insight into the individual who lives there. If there are beer cans and cigarettes, maybe you have a bad renter or someone who does not have the pride of ownership. A lack of upgrades is something I would see in a home where the owners have lived there from the beginning of time. Especially if it is in a neighborhood where everyone has well-manicured lawns and clean driveways. Then you walk up to a home where there are a few old cars that look like they never move or maybe even an engine missing. You can build an impression of the kind of occupant that is there. Often it is someone who will never sell or move because they have been there forever and maybe have the home paid for.

There will be homes you approach that have a small sign that read *"Nana and Papa live here."* The home could be well cared for and maybe even have a ramp leading to the front door. You can then assume that an elderly couple live there. What if you also notice that it is a two story property? Now as you approach, you may deal with an elderly couple who are only using the bottom part of the home and are often chatting about getting into a one story. Maybe when you walk up the other spouse has passed and one of them is considering a move to a home or a senior community. You can gather a ton of information from the approach.

A home with a pile of shoes at the door point to several different cultures and also alert you to take your shoes off before you enter. A home with a ton of kids' toys and bikes show a family and depending on the toys can reveal several boys and girls of different ages. Should this home be a shoe box size with no yard, this may be a reason for them to want a bigger home. A home with a small trash can full of other agents propaganda may mean they expect you to know you are probably delivering trash. Seeing real estate signs in an open garage may show an agent lives there. Seeing a lock box but no sign may be a recent sale or a fresh listing. A pile of newspapers may show a vacant home along with hearing a smoke alarm chirping. I once got a listing by noticing that a lawn was way too dead for that neighborhood. There was also a few marketing pieces from solar companies, landscapers and maids piled up at the door. I knocked on the door and no one was home. I looked up their number and called the owner. It turned out it was a divorce, and they just walked away and neither of them want the home. I got the listing that night? This is rare, but having this happen says that it could happen again. If I just look for clues and potential signs of motivating factors.

Walking up to a home with storage pods in the driveway is an indicator of potential moves. I have gotten deals from walking up to a home that was having the house painted. If you see a garage sale happening, you should stop and ask if they are interested in selling. Having a construction crew or a dumpster is a good indicator of major events happening in the home.

One of the approach standards I have adopted is with a courtyard. This is a small gate that you have to open before you get to the front door. I used to feel like if that gate was taller than my chest I would not even bother and skip that home. Now I am lowering my bar just like I lower the gate height. If the gate is below my waist, I might open it. However, this borders on trespassing. Aware of the approach, I am also looking for signs that this little gate is meant to hold back a dog. If the owner is used to opening the door because they assume the gate is closed then it is also possible that the dog will feel the same. Then if the door opens, and the gate is open either the dog runs away or it eats you. This is your call how you want to handle gates. I once had a guy walking across the street as I was opening a small gate and I heard him say. *"That is probably closed for a reason."* It stuck with me. If I see a small gate but cannot see whether there is a dog possible I just walk on by. Sometimes I will go into the gate but if it is close enough to the door, I will walk up and ring the bell and then step back behind that gate just in case.

Chapter Five
At the Door

A lead is an individual who can say "No" but they don't.
A contact is an individual who can say "no" but maybe they don't.-Me

There are thousands of scripts and dialogues on the internet. Each one of them work. When I listen to them though I often find myself face palming. There are so many things you have to say in a conversation and so many you should not.

The aim at the door serves three objectives. The three are in a question format to keep it simple. It is to keep you on track. If the individual is conversational, then chat away. Remember, you got 2 ears and one mouth for a reason. To listen twice as much as you talk. Questions are a good way to keep conversations around the prospect instead of you. People love to talk about themselves.

Objective number One. Do I have a lead? The answer is yes or no. The way it sounds to your ears is no or maybe not. If the individual in question is reluctant, then you *must* ask the followup question. *"Do you think maybe later down the road, like next spring?* You should insert a future date or season that makes sense to you. Also, the reason I ask it this way is that when confronted by having to decide about a purchase or move most people are not comfortable answering this at the moment. But if you push it out to a place far away from the need to stress about it now, then they will more often than not give you a maybe still. Tony Robbins says that the fear of loss is greater than the thought of gain or something to that effect. What I'm doing here is causing a bit of pain, because moving is never pleasurable, and then letting off of that pressure point by making it something they can deal with later. This is especially true from October to January because the holidays are the only thing on peoples minds. Even though the holidays comprise maybe of 96 hours of down time between Thanksgiving, Christmas Eve and Day and New Years. Regardless, this is exactly what you are looking for. Remember this, and I quote myself. A lead is an individual who can say *"no"* but they don't. A contact is an individual who can say *"no"* but maybe they don't.

Objective number two. When will they act? It is very rare in the real estate industry to find someone who is ready to list their home on the spot. In other industries like pest companies, solar companies and door-to-door product sales you need to close right there and then, because you may never return to that community. Actually, solar companies and pest companies and even any company who deals with a geographical region with limits on how far they will prospect would benefit from asking the "maybe later close." That way you can go back for a sale or at least generate a contact record for follow up. I think I have had less than 10 unicorn leads over my years. That does not mean that you will not find them, it just means that they are rare. Having the right expectation will help you not be frustrated when you are at door number 3,999. I use this number because I have found a strange coincidence that when I reach around 4,000 doors, I find someone who I get under contract within 7 days of our first meeting. Finding out when they will act on the sale will help you with number three.

Objective number three. If not now, when? Follow up. Without lead generation you have nothing. Without follow up you get nothing. That's another Festini-ism. If you are at the door and you can tell this is not going as planned but you know that later you will get the sale then it is critical that you gather information right there and then. Otherwise, you can never follow up unless you look them up online to call them or take the time to go back to the door. Either of these is a risk of losing the opportunity to build the relationship. The sole purpose of my going to the door is to build a relationship with a potential customer as fast as possible before they decide on someone to hire. Once they know, like and trust me, I will have them as a customer for life and as long as I provide value I am golden. If you are in a business that requires getting the order right on the spot then step three is just get the order, set an appointment.

The key pieces of information I want are a time line, a phone number and an email address. I do not need not ask for the name because I have access to that. Often you find that when they give you their email address, it will include a name in the address. Like jamesfestini@gmail.com. At that point I will ask, *"I assume your are James?"* and they will reply. Depending on their motivation will depend on how I implement my effective follow-up campaign comprising the 5 marketing methods spelled out in the chapter on 5 marketing methods.

"I am a human lie detector in a controlled environment" -Me

In 2014 Time Magazine produced an article along with studies from Microsoft on the attention span of humans in the modern age of tech. The results showed that it is now at the level of a goldfish. Have you heard this before? This was in 2015. The study also states that it was 12 seconds in the year 2000. Imagine what it could be by the time you are consuming this content. Eight seconds to capture the attention of the consumer and get your desired outcome would be impossible if your expectations required more time to establish rapport and trust and close. I have also seen many articles from places like Forbes and Inc. that suggest that humans form first impressions in 7 seconds. I have a few theories on these time lines as they apply to our sales efforts.

Since we are dealing with outbound efforts, I often talk about the phones, and how I use this style as it applies almost the same as it would to door-to-door. There is a reason my script is so short. It is that I do not want the consumer to think about their answer. It is so I can read and interpret the "knee jerk" response. For nearly 30 years I have been repeating the same script but I never really gave it any thought why it was effective or why it was so simple. Once I began sharing my methods, I began having people question the style and rhythm. I need to be very clear that this will be during a cold door and not during a follow up call or with anyone who may know me or have shown an interest in selling ever. That way we can be realistic in the expectation of a result.

I enter the call knowing that I have less than eight seconds to achieve one thing. It is not to establish rapport as most sales trainer would have you believe. It is not to smile when I dial and let them hear my enthusiasm like the "sales gurus" may have taught you. Why not?

To understand this you must first understand consumer acquisition using the active sales methods and the evolution in this genre. Cold Calling and door to door sales. Since the late 1990s, caller ID was something only a few who had a special phone to read this data. So most people would pick up the phone. Telemarketers were not as abundant as they became only ten years later. What happened? Outsourcing and expansion to other countries and boiler rooms with massive technologies to dial hundreds of thousands of numbers. It got so bad that by 2003 the United States implemented a do not call list. Millions registered and by my estimation it took the telephone lists we had down to 30% of what could once be dialed.

Then several years later smart phones came on the scene with a caller ID on every phone. This technological leap in evolution coupled with sophisticated applications that blocked unwanted calls made it even harder to connect with the consumer. Especially the consumer that did not know us and could not identify us before they answered.

Now imagine you are sitting at the park with your kid and a phone call comes in. You do not recognize the number but you answer anyway. The voice on the other line sounds enthusiastic as they asks if they are speaking with the right person or the decision maker. Perhaps they break in the call with an overly friendly audible of your name as if you have known each other for years but asks if it is you at the same time. You immediately hear the sounds of the background of other callers and within seconds identify this as a telemarketer in a boiler room. You are polite so they keep talking. All the while you are forming the guts to say no the second you find it convenient enough or maybe you just hang up. Within 8 seconds you have decided that all you want to do is get off the phone and you should have never answered it. Because you are not interested. This is with a caller ID and a number you do not know. What if your phone identifies the call as "spam" or "robo-caller?" as many now do. You don't even answer. You swipe left. I am going out on a limb to say the the telemarketing industry is on life support and could slip into a coma by 2022 and the plug be pulled by 2025. Yes, the death of the telemarketing industry. When the do not call list arrived it killed 70% of our numbers and this was in the hands of the FCC. Buy 2010 the do not call list was more of a joke because we still got the sales calls even though we registered our number. In 2019, the FCC implemented technologies to put the power of call blocking and telemarketing warfare into the hands of any consumer with a smart phone. Making pick up rates plummet, coupled with the swipe left

73

society, soon we will not be able to call anyone without them having to know who we are. As of this writing, most people I know say they never answer a call from a number they do not know.

Now as society, we do not have the brain of a goldfish or that we are as dumb as our water loving friends. It is that with the emergence of technology and the speed at which our information is coming at us; we have to decide a lot faster than we used to. When we are put in a position to make a judgment on what we perceive to be annoying or what we deem valuable will be based on a comfort level for *that* moment. Maybe you have made one of these calls and had a great and very long and productive chat on a Monday and the consumer says call back Friday to set an appointment. When you call back you get into the introduction and they just hang up. Have you had that? If not, then you have not made enough calls. It is the weirdest thing, but it happens to me all the time. Often it is because I go into the callback with that excited familiar voice that sales trainers teach most salespeople, and with good reason because we became friends on Monday, only to have them completely forget we ever spoke. It is because that call was at the right time and this call was not. Believe me when I say I would call back the following Monday and go in with my cold intro script, have them take the bait, and then immediately say in a *"oh man that's right, we talked last week"* and have them kick right back into friend zone.

Not that they were meaning to be rude but that we are becoming a society of individuals who have no problem being dismissive and when being rude becomes the societal norm, I suppose it's no longer rude but in a way it is. We are quick to distinguish between not right now and never. As salespeople we understand that often an individual who says maybe *today* may also be a *not right now* but *maybe later when I am ready*. This is where my script fits in.

Lets look at the mind of a consumer in those 8 seconds.

0 Second- a call comes in and they think to themselves *"I have no idea who this is."* They think *"maybe a telemarketer. I'll answer, but it better be good."*

1-5 *Seconds*-HELLO? Listens to the sounds on the phone, *the caller asks if this is me? Of Course it is me, it is my phone, Ugh, not another salesperson.*

6-15 *Seconds*-Listens to a very enthusiastic individual speaking too fast and not getting to the point. *I wonder if I left the coffeepot on* (8 Seconds is up)

6-20 *Seconds- I am kind of creeped out at how they are pretending to give a crap and as soon as they shut up I am going to say no.* "NO I'm not interested."

Hopefully, any time past that is not spent in frustration at the caller because they won't get off the phone. Immediately and frequently these consumers are being conditioned to think and respond with this attitude and as the calls come in more and more they become less and less interested. Even if they are interested, it is highly likely that the potential customer checked out before they even know what the call was about.

Picture an imaginary brick wall, being built by the consumer during the first contact, its being built complete with sound proofing and every second represents brick layers 5 inches high. Now imagine the person building this wall is the consumer and the salesperson is just on the other side of this wall. Now imagine that you have less than eight seconds to capture their attention, tell them who you are and why you are calling AND get them to reveal their interest in your product or service before you are completely behind their defensive wall. What would you say in this situation?

Let's go through this scenario using my script and what the consumer might be thinking at the door.

0 second- Doorbell rings. *Did I order a package? Who can it be?* Lets assume they are also busy and are not expecting to be taken away from whatever else was probably more important.

1-3 Seconds- The door opens and they think to themselves *"I have no idea who this is,maybe a friend or foe, they seem harmless, who are they and what do they want?"*

3-6 seconds into the meeting. Now they know my name, my company and my purpose.

7-8 seconds into the conversation. I hit them with a very direct question. *Oh, real estate. What does this have to do with me?* (If they are not interested they say no, but if they are interested) *Actually, I am thinking of selling or moving, this is an odd coincidence but I am kind of busy.*

Here is where it gets interesting. If they are not thinking of selling at all, I will hear them say *"no"* by pronouncing the word N.O. I will see their body say the same. If they are thinking of selling but not at this time, half of the time they will say *"no"* and the other half of the time they will say *"nah"* with a long drag in their answer. If they say *"no"* but think "yes," I can pick up on that slight inflection in their voice. It will sound like an "uncertain no". It will sound like someone who is thinking *"not right now but maybe later."* I know it seems strange to be "able to hear" a *"maybe"* or even a *"yes"* when they said *"no"*, but I assure you that if you tune your ear, you will hear it. Just like a musician can tell the difference between a minor and major key, I have tuned my ear to listen to subtle variations in how someone says *"no"* that I can pick up on it. But, just like a musician you must practice listening to the notes in a song to identify over time exactly where that note is and what it was. Fortunately, I can teach this much easier than it is to learn music. I sometimes refer to this as being a human lie detector, but maybe it is more like being a human "hiding the truth" detector.

Let's address what I know most salespeople would say. That the "knee jerk" response will always be "no." The "knee jerk" phrase comes from the medical world and is actually called "patella tendon reflex test," where a doctor has the patient sit on a table and he hits the tendon just below the kneecap with a triangle rock. If the patient's reflexes are healthy, the lower leg will jerk forward. If they are not, the knee may jerk a bit but not as much. To the untrained eye the professional is just hitting a leg. To the doctor this knee jerk is the different between life and death. I am just kidding, it means something though. Using my scripts without being trained on the response variables would be like trying to put a 1,000 piece puzzle together without the picture. Sure you might figure it out but why go through the struggle?

So what can one do with knowing that everybody says "no?" Learn the subtle yet distinct variations of *"no"* that means *"not right now"* which is often *"maybe"* and even *"yes."* Expecting someone to say *"yes"* is ambitious when you ask a question that requires a yes or no answer to such a big life decision as moving. In any other field of door-to-door sales you might have to play with ways to force a response out of a prospect that would be consistent enough to practice listening for ways that they can hint at possibility.

Just like the variations of accents in America can say the same series of words that are written on paper and be read out loud, once heard there is a difference. I can spot accents inside of the sounds and with my hundreds maybe thousands of hours of intentional listening. Often, I am able to discern what country that accent is from. So can you too learn to identify when an individual is saying *"no"* and thinking *"yes."* It is significantly easier to hear this in person where you can read body language as well. Like at the door.

Your dance is body language and your music is words.-Me

This may all be very difficult to describe and to understand body language by reading without seeing me. I will do my best to break it down. Your body is a two-part instrument that composes music. This music is vast and varied in its complexities from a large orchestra to a hand clap. Each presentation you make is a short song or a concert. You must be good at adjusting the volume and tempo along with the genre itself. It's a little bit country and it's a little bit rock n' roll. Like when you enter someone's vehicle and demand to be the DJ on a short or long trip this would require you to compromise and if you have ever done this with someone you know how hard it can be. I cannot stand it when my wife is the DJ. She is a today's hits and I am an almost everything but. Just do not play country, bluegrass is where I draw the line. Now amplify this theory with a stranger who is already reluctant to answer the door, if they do, you are a salesperson, yuck, and you have likely interrupted something far more important to play terrible country music at their door as you break dance. How is that for imagination?

If you can learn to adjust your persona to be acceptable to many, you will get far as a door-to-door salesperson. Your dancing is body language and your music is your words. From the moment you are within eye shot of the potential prospect you are on stage. You must make this the performance of a lifetime each time. I realize this is extreme. Unless you have gone to the door before and had one of these "once in a lifetime" performances. Like Queen at Live-Aid. One where everything you said was impeccable, and the prospect loved everything you said and you landed the deal. Where you walked away not walking but floating off of the driveway. Just as you might have also experienced the opposite. One where you somehow forgot how to speak your native language and the potential client looks at you like you just farted and was completely repulsed and confused at the same time. Worse is that as you walked away, you knew that was a lead and you choked.

If you have never been to a door, then it is highly likely that your first door will either feel like this or you will fear even trying because of this very unlikely scenario. I promise you that as you do more doors, you will get better. It is like learning to play an instrument. Nobody picks up an instrument and plays. They fumble, then fiddle, then they practice, then they noodle, then they jam or shred. I am convinced that within 10 doors your fears will completely disappear. My problem to this day is not the fear of knocking but the reluctance because of complacency. Once I am at the first door though I can go for hours. You just have to go through the motions. Work out the cobwebs and kinks in your delivery both with your body gestures and with your words as they are delivered.

I have showed this style on video and in seminars and each time I display what I am saying and how I say it I am often comparing it to the world's greatest athletes. One where each frame is dissected to unlock the secrets to how they differ from every other person in their game. What do they do with their wrist for a golfer and what they do with their eyes for a quarterback? Like a great chess player we calculate each move with precision and an expectation of winning based on experience and knowing outcomes. You probably thought this is a joke, right? James is comparing himself to Tiger Woods, Kobe Bryant and Drew Brees? For door-to-door sales? A bit. When I describe the process of every eyebrow raise and each shoulder jerk and hand gesture, it is not because I am making it up as I go but that I am performing it from muscle memory. That's why I love door knocking over calling on the phone. Over the phone all you have is your voice at the door I can perform.

We are getting ahead of ourselves. Let's go back to somewhere between the stealth drop and the approach. Assuming that you are being watched or that you pay attention as you move through space you will carry yourself with a straight and comfortable posture. If you slouch, then slouch less. If you are a foot dragger, then drag less. Have you ever watched American Idol or Shark Tank? Those first few moments before the presenter opens their mouth, the judges are already murmuring words of judgment. Whispering words of their impressions of the presenter. This is human nature. Back in our caveman days just a few thousand years ago we were programmed to distinguish and decide if this was friend or foe within seconds. The way you carry your body across the street and onto the sidewalk and up to the door matters. Assume you are being watched. That way when they open the door the perk up is less obvious.

You walk up, your stealth drop was made and you ring the bell. It is critical that you give a person space. It is called personal space. Everyone has their own personal space depending on the situation. If they are at a concert or theme park its arms' length. Sometimes less. If they are in a park, it's probably about 10 feet with a stranger passing by and 10 inches with a friend or family. At the door, on their turf, and depending on the neighborhood, and we must understand the character of the individual and their defensible space. Meaning that you are not in a public place but in fact encroaching on their property and assumed a threat.. Not that every person will assume you are a serial killer but there is that nature or nurture, fight or flight, village protections underlying in each of us when someone approaches that package that we protect. Our home. The place where I store my love and possessions and now you are here to do what?

This ideal space is about 5-7 feet depending on the architecture of the home. If there is an entryway with 7 stairs to the door mat, then the bottom of those steps are OK. It is almost a distance far enough that if an attacker was to charge at the door, they could react and lock it. Make sense? If there is a screen door that you cannot see them but they see you, then this distance is still about 5-7 feet. This will always be far enough away to deliver your pitch without having to cross that shouting threshold. If they are hard of hearing you may have to step in and speak up. I have on occasion, been asked to step closer and that "they don't bite." This is how far back I am. I want the individual to see my entire body because I am using this as a tool to convey that I am not a threat and that I can be heard and trusted as a professional businessperson. I spoke in depth on the Ring doorbell in another chapter, but different from a bell is a peephole. These old holes in the door can see about 5 feet with distorted clarity so again about 7 feet to display your whole body. Often this peephole is followed up with a "who is it?" from someone who will not be opening the door half the time. So you must speak loud enough to talk through the 2 inches wood. If they are interested, they might open the door. Just because they open the door does not mean they are interested, it could just mean they needed clarity of the situation or maybe to see and hear you better. This may lead to repeating the entire pitch from the start when they are now looking at you.

There will be times that the door is wide open and you do not see anyone. Then ring the bell, knock if you don't hear a bell, and step back a bit farther. It is a good possibility that the occupant forgot to close the door or that they will be walking from a distance in the back ground to get to the doorway. This is a very uncomfortable evolutionary vibe that you are closer to the door than they are and must move faster to get to the defensive location. This may not be obvious but this is in us. If you see that they see you but have to approach from afar I take a small step back to subliminally position myself in a subordinate position. Man this is weird to try to describe. Body language is the apes and animals in the wild. It is millions of years of evolution. This is why I use these words to describe my gestures as subtle but significant. This has evolved to be called NLP or neuro-linguistic programming. A topic covered in another chapter.

When I am delivering the script and it is the first line, it is usually on the offense. I am out of the blue asking them if they have an interest in making a decision right now. When they respond I will subtly step back with one leg just a hair to convey a message of I am leaving now and there is no need to put up your defenses, they read this as he is leaving now, and that is when I hit them with the Columbo Close if I sense it is needed. If not, then I am out of there. If the Columbo works, then I must go back to the offense and ask if they are thinking of maybe later. When I deliver this maybe later wording I am putting my hand out and doing a so-so maybe not, hand movement as if am still slightly positioned in a *"am about to leave"* body signal with the shoulders twisting a bit but feet in place. If they are a lead, they will open up. If they are not, I will sense this is and proceed with a goodbye. Each one is different but I am going on a maybe still. The next delivery is my subliminal offer to give them a function of my services that they likely have already using the internet to acquire.

The next question is designed to ask if they have any idea what the home is worth? Solar companies ask what they think they could save having solar? Pest control would ask if they have seen any bugs or wood damage? This question is a team effort to engage the person in a mutual project that they might have done and you also do for a living. Sometimes they will say that they know what it is worth and maybe even say the price along with the source. If the source is an agent, then that is an upcoming objection. If the source is an online algorithm, I pay attention to how they say, "Well Zilliasstimate says $XXX,XXX." I made up that word. They tell me the price and I ask what do they think about that? This is to see if this price is good or bad. If it is a good price, they will respond with a bit of pleasure, but if it is bad, you will hear it. Either way, this dialog is carefully crafted and delivered to get to the 2nd and 3rd objectives spelled out in the 3 objectives chapter. Identify if I have a lead, asses motivation, get contact information for follow up if no close happens now.

I don't know what I can say about some people who have strange speaking habits and gesture with too much or too little movement. I am not talking medical conditions here; I am talking about being awkward. The only way to get past your idiosyncrasies is to face someone at the door about 1,000 times. I think maybe 10,000 doors might exorcise that demon that possesses you to be cringey or creepy. If you are naturally quirky or spicy, then this is OK because most people will be attracted to your personality. But if you have the personality of a dirt bag or you put off a serial killer vibe, then you may seriously need to polish your delivery and character. I don't mean that if you have a face meant for radio or look like you were weened on a pickle or even if you look like Willem Dafoe, you can be pleasing in your smile and energy. I don't mean to pick on Willem but besides Tommy Lee Jones; I can't think of an actor more unapproachable on first impressions than they would be at the door. You can practice your face and sounds in the mirror. If you need some personal hygiene tips or see your reflection and you don't like it, fix it. If it is something you were born with then own it. There is a difference between having a personality and having an appearance. You can work on your appearance and you can always improve your personality. Be friendly and approachable.

One odd thing I try to do during my door knocking is to think in my head, "I Love You." This may not work for some of you if you are staring like "I want you" rather than "I love you." But if I try to project a sincere love from my heart, even if it not love, it makes a world of difference. People have a hard time being jerks to kind, sympathetic people. This is how I often convert total jerks into pleasant conversations. By being agreeable and kind, courteous, succinct, well spoken and calm. This happens with my words and my actions. Body language speaks volume but when accompanied by kind words it amplifies body language. I would suggest you watch programs like Shark Tank or Ted Talks to spot the differences in personalities that try to deliver their message. You will form an opinion of those who have it together and those who do not in the first seconds then change your opinions as they speak. These are great examples of being able to watch someone on the approach and the first 8 seconds.

My script introduces, know, my smile says I am a kind, like, and my body says they can trust me. -Me

Have you heard of NLP aka Neuro-linguistic programming? How about mirroring and matching? Maybe you know these terms as building rapport. Maybe you just know it as being friendly and getting along. We can study the science behind the NLP technology by a well known master of this science, the self-help guru Tony Robbins. Although he was not the founder of this, he made it mainstream. Basically, when you are in a one-on-one situation, we behave in an unspoken or spoken dance of the 5 senses. Imagine if you are in a foreign country where no one speaks your language and then you meet that one person that does. That person is your new best friend. Even if they are a little bit country and you are a little bit rock n' roll. It is a connection that finds familiarity through body signals and words spoken that makes you feel like I can trust this person. The oldest adage in sales is that they have to know like and trust you. My script introduces, know, my smile says I am a kind, like, and my body says they can trust me. Sure it is not a full blown relationship, but it is just enough to win over the prospect if they are interested and get the ones who are not interested to drop their guard long enough to determine if they are telling the truth or not.

The line of sight is also a factor in NLP. Sometimes there is a bush or a fence in the way. There are these houses I come across where the front door is on the side of the house like where most garage side doors are and the threshold is only about 3 feet wide. This design goes against everything I am comfortable relating to *in line of sight and personal space.* Sometimes there is even a long corridor of trees that make it dark so now I am just 3 feet away. In this situation I step back far enough so they see me and sometimes they have to open the door a bit and pop their head out to talk. This will be a situational thing, but now you know how I handle it.

The distance from the door can be measured at about three or four steps back. You should pay attention to that few steps back. Because although I have not fallen on my butt I have stumbled backwards right in front of the occupant, so much so they say, *"oh, be careful"* or *"watch your step."* It pays to have a script handy for these situations. Here is mine on the ready for when it happens. *'I'm and a trained professional, don't try this at home,"* or perhaps *"I do my own stunts kids don't try this at home."* Please if you break something on your body walk away as best you can. Don't make them play nurse or doctor and call an ambulance. That would suck. If you break something of theirs than that is awkward. I cover this in the book just in case.

What if you have something to your appearance that cannot be avoided? On one extreme you are a Sikh or a Muslim and your religion is on your head or obvious in your appearance and you work in an area that may be sensitive to cultural differences. Discrimination. There, I said it. Honestly, we should be allowed to discriminate with respect and not be disrespectful racists. We judge by nature and try to sugarcoat it with acceptance and diversity. I have nothing against anyone. You do you. However, if you come into my line of sight, I will form an impression based on my experience and opinion formed though my upbringing and cultural surrounding in my life. If this is the case, then I would strongly suggest that your words are impeccable with an accent that reveals your heritage at about a 10% thickness. I am not suggesting you eliminate your accent and abandon your religion. I can only point to the newscasters in the world. No matter what race and origin they appear to be, they all speak the same way. Even in the United States, the ones behind the news desk rarely have an accent. Except for the ones who go out on location. I'll bet you didn't notice. If you were born with another language in the home, and you left that language as a primary after you turned 16 years old, you are probably stuck with an accent. Especially if this primary language is still spoken at home. Work on proper pronunciation take your accent from a ten to a two. Just enough to make you special but not so much that is is a hindrance to acceptance. Sometimes I hear a sloppy Indian accent and its gross and then I will hear a well spoken Indian accent and its hot. Same country and region, different delivery. Study your native people that are on public platforms who deliver words with eloquence and practice. A foreign accent delivered with confidence is powerful. Use it and do not let it be a hindrance. Fair Enough?

What if you are physically varied like a wearing a turban, or have facial deformities, scars or a serious limp? Own it. You are who you are. If you are comfortable enough to read this book, then you are open to showing who you are to lots of people and this was never a problem. But what if this is still an underlying issue? Again do your best and own it. Play on your strengths and have them camouflage your weakness so that the only thing the prospect thinks is oh poor you, then oh wow they are well spoken and carry themselves well. Again, this may work to your advantage. If it is a limp, try to get stronger or really try to correct as best you can. I cannot speak for this so to each their own. I can only observe and compare people who have had similar amputations. One will train hard and you would never see it unless they exposed it and the other will walk with a limp. The difference may only be how hard they worked and continue to work on their mobility so as not not be judged or stand out in a critical society.

In high school, that was long ago, way before prosthetics advanced, I had an acquaintance that had a very, very slight limp but I never asked. Then one day we played kick ball, and he had to kick and run. Let's just say high school can be a cruel place and so is the world still. Brush it off and own it. Work on it. I know a lady in real estate that has a prosthetic arm. She wore coats and carried herself well. I have a friend with a glass eye and I have seen business cards with eye patches and sure it is a double take but that's it. I have also seen business cards where the photo looks like a terrorist mugshot complete with no smile at all and white background and turban. I love the Sikhs above many other cultures so don't get me wrong on this. If that guy just smiled, I would not have even written that last sentence. It was just that look on his face like he hated the camera. Why doesn't anyone step in and help? Well here I am. Telling you the truth. You are too fat; you are too thin; you are too dark; you are too light and for sure you are too foreign and too local.

I say I am vanilla and so are you yet we are two different vanillas. One is vanilla plain old vanilla, like the one in ice cream sandwiches. The other is vanilla bean and has a bit of a bite if its real vanilla bean, my preferred vanilla. My kids hate vanilla bean but love vanilla. Maybe I, James Festini, can be more vanilla in America, and you cannot help being vanilla bean. We are still vanilla. If we will go out into the world and try to meet the standards of everybody we try to pitch, we can go as vanilla but carry a large variety of cherries, bananas, chocolate, caramel, nuts, and whip cream to accommodate the tastes of most. Let your words be your character and your actions be your reputation. I would use cheese or beer for this vanilla analogy but I think that would have failed. I would use wine but what the hell do I know about wine. I like the boxed chillable red and I hear that stuff is crap to the wine aficionados. Aren't you glad I made you a sundae?

A few words on rapport building. Have you ever seen the movie Glengarry Glen Ross? If you have not, then go see it. Anyhow, there is a scene in there where Sheldon "The Machine" Levine, played by the late great Jack Lemmon, is a desperate salesman in need of a sale. He shows up at a door unannounced in the rain and pretty much invites himself in. He immediately grabs a fishing rod and starts trying to small talk about fishing, along with other embellishments and ramblings to gain a personal connection with the potential customer. In this scene it ends with a terrible prospect with no need or qualifications. He would have been better off door knocking instead of waiting around the office. This scene is an example of how not to to build rapport. Rapport is a slow and subtle connection made by finding things in common along with identifying unspoken similarities such as body types, facial features and body gestures. Some would say that if a person opens the door and they are talking with a southern accent that you also talk with a southern accent. This is extreme and if they notice it you went too far. Rather, you can use terms familiar with the region, if you are familiar with that.

For example, I am from Peru and we refer the form of Spanish spoken there as Castillian, and to the trained ear you hear that they are probably from South America and maybe Spain. This is until they say something with an "s" and pronounce it as "th" then it's Spain for sure. Anyhow, there are often moments that I pick up on that and when they say a country anywhere in South America, it's like with are related because we are not as common around here. Then we talk food and restaurants and boom, I am family. If you see a kid about the size and shape of your kid, you can talk about schools. Often I say, *"hey your kid looks like the size and age of mine. What are they like 9?"* Word of caution, this can be creepy so if you are naturally or physically creepy in appearance and mannerisms and have not mastered being vanilla I would stay away from this one and all talk of children. Unless you actually have them.

I drive a Mercedes Benz Sprinter and I used to drive a Hummer. I was in the Army and Graduated from the local high school. These are easily spotted in the approach when you see a car in the driveway or a sticker on the window of the school or military pride. I say hey I was 11 Bravo and if they are military, they know that means my job sucked. It meant infantry. Lots of crawling in the mud, shooting guns and walking in the dark for days. A real conversation piece versus if I was a cook or mechanic. Although flight and tank mechanics have stories. I have also run seven marathons and completed several centuries on the bike. I have to add a marathon is always 26.2 miles, and a Century is 100 because to those of who have done these, we cringe when someone calls a run a marathon if it is not a full 26.2 miles. It's a half marathon or 10k or something else. If I see they are wearing an Ironman shirt or have the honorable "M-Dot, a word used to describe the logo for the event known as Ironman, I will comment with an, "oh man did you do it?" To which they will clarify a half or a full along with dates, locations and times. It's and endurance athlete thing to do this but you really can get them chatting if you are genuinely interested because this is your world too. It is not that hard to find common ground but if there is none then don't try so hard. A smile and politeness will do just fine.

If you notice one thing in common with each of these instances, is that I am looking for opportunities for people to talk about themselves and not about me or my goods. This will happen at the right moment and can not be taught but we can practice it. Also, these moments are opportunities to share enthusiasm and excitement about them and this will transition over to your pitch when the chit chat is done. I am thinking about the solar panel kid who goes to each door doing a "Sheldon Levine" on the fly at all doors because they have to close there and then. I get that building speed rapport matters but faking an interest is easily spotted. Find common ground. If you can't then work on your faking this, but I will see through it. I see it and I hear it. Therefore, when I train people to door knock, I suggest they go in vanilla and add the toppings if the conversation carries on past the rejection. Even then a rejection read as a "no" is still a no. That means rapport game over. Move on. Rapport is used to gain trust so that the customer will let their guard down and allow you to engage them if they need your service. We build sales on finding a need and filling it. Sometimes this need is a cause of pain and sometimes it is a need to gain pleasure. Neither of these will reveal themselves until they let you into their world.

"Oh, there's just one more thing"-Columbo

Have you ever watched the TV show Columbo? If you have not, it is no big loss. I have a hard time with most everything that came out of the 70s except for The Fonz and The Godfather. Detective Columbo was about an LAPD gumshoe with a goofy and quirky style, played by Peter Falk. The story would always start out with a crime and then turn into a "who done it" drama. The detective would stumble around the crime scene and among criminals pretending to be friendly and asking questions of those around the crime. He would sometimes ask completely off the wall questions to draw out some revealing answers. Many times Columbo knew who committed the crime long before the show was ending. But in the most classical Columbo way, he would converse with the suspect in a relaxed tone until the right moment where he would ask the criminal a question that would incriminate them. What he did was leading them to the truth without letting them know that they were being baited into a confession. He would allow them to take down their guard by connecting with them in a manor that made the person comfortable to talk. Most of the time it was his sloppy appearance and clueless demeanor that would have the criminal believing that this detective person was a harmless idiot.

In sales, the individual may or may not be guilty of wanting our product or service. Most times we may not have the time to interrogate them. More often than not the potential customer is too busy and even though they may be ready to transact, it may not be right now. It is our job to ask the most important question up front so we can identify a lead. We must act as a "human lie detector" by listening carefully to the way they answer our questions. We have to listen carefully to how they say no. In person we must observe body language that suggests discomfort and be willing to step away from that confrontation to put them at ease.

Columbo could ask a question or mention a detail of the crime and watch as the criminal reacted to hitting that nerve. We too can see whether we are on to something and then know to change the inquisition to not only a subordinate position but almost a cowardly retreat. This is most obvious when we are on a cold call or a cold door. An individual who has no clue who we are or what our call is about. On the phone we will ask if they are interested right away. If we sense that they are reluctant in their response with a "soft" no, then we must ask the follow up question. The follow up question must be one that disarms the contact so they do not feel as if they are about to be sold.

Here is how the conversation would go in a real estate situation.

Prospect: *Hello?*

Agent: *Hi my name is Agent with Company and I was wondering if you might be interested in selling your house?*

Prospect: *Nah* (with that spike in your lie detector you hear reluctance)

Agent: *Well, do you think maybe later down the road you might reconsider, maybe (season)?*

Prospect: *Perhaps I'm not sure. We have kids graduating, retirement, etc.*

Agent: *Do you have any idea what the home is worth?* (as your body and eyes scan the architecture and eaves in an appraising manner)

Prospect: *No/Yes* (doesn't matter)

Agent: *Would it be OK if I could email you some comps or sales in the area, that way later when you are ready you might think of me and have my information. It's no problem… what's a good email?*

Prospect: *8 out of ten times they give it,* (then small talk)

Agent: *Thank you very much for your time and we will keep in touch. Have a great day.*

If you noticed the moment after the prospect reluctantly rejects the pitch, the agent did not go in for a close or ask a question that would shut down the prospect and keep them in full defense mode. They have already revealed just enough to not know that they give up control of in the interaction. We must always make the prospect feel in control. Even if saying no is their way of controlling the outcome and ending the effort to get the sale. This is the exact opposite of most sales trainer's suggestions. They say always take control. Say their name because people like to hear their name. The problem with that is that you may have the wrong name or person, and even if you do, you can't know if they go by Mr., Mrs, Miss, Jim, James, Jimmy or even Jimbo. The odds are that you will say something to repel rather than neutralize. The best thing you can do is back off. They rejected you in their mind. They said no. You heard maybe. So why not throw the maybe out there and place the time of sale way off into the future where they control when they will be ready. When you ask them *"maybe later down the road?"* it is critical you say it with a tone that sounds like a drawn out song like tone that places it far away. Stressing the "ay" in *"maybe."*In person you can even shift backwards in a walk away posture and use your hands in a "so-so" palm twist to deliver a not sure hand signal that would lure the answer you seek. It's hard to describe this but I hope you get it.

These actions and words may seem like casual conversation, but to the trained individual it is exactly what you must do each time. Just like Columbo appears a bit confused to the perpetrator, so the individual can let their guard down and open themselves for the critical question that will incriminate themselves. Columbo would step away and turn back to say,*"just one more question."* This would be the question that would nail the suspect to the crime.

Obviously we are not really cops and the prospect is not lying, we will always have this conversation at the wrong time so we have to extract the objectives and leave before they reject you. The odds of them being able to chat about it in that moment is rare. Depending on the product. If there is a drought and you are selling water, it is likely you will find lots of motivated individuals. If you are in a tech convention hosting a booth and the individual passes by, you might see the hesitation of those who may or may not see something they like just by witnessing a double glance at your booth. If you are a car salesperson and you see someone walk on the lot and go straight to the 4-door sedan and walk around, you may have a clue what the want. When the prospect comes to you or by you, you have an advantage. It is more of an inbound inquiry than an outbound cold call but to the trained salesperson, you can convert this to a sale.

Fortunately, in real estate, I know where the product is. It is fixed to the ground and connected by pipes and wires with a roof on top.

Therefore, all we need to do is walk up to the product and ask if the person standing on it might want to sell it. If we do this on their turf and on their schedule, it is up to us to find out when would be a good time. By asking for an email address, or phone number, I can walk away for the moment with something that I can use to follow up. Columbo gets what he needs to say *"you have the right to remain silent."* It is up to the judge and jury to decide if they are guilty. We have enough to say you are a lead. It is up to our follow up to know if they are motivated to sign a contract.

"I want 100% of their attention to be on my 8 second question."
-Me

Have you ever heard someone say that when taking a lie detector test that one could put a thumbtack in their shoe so that when asked that question that would incriminate them, they could step on the tack and trick the test? I'm not sure where I heard this but I know what that means for door knocking.

My script and approach requires that you develop a sixth sense when at the door. That when you ask the individual if they are interested and they respond with a "reluctant no", you can pick up on subtle but distinct variation in tone and body language that should lead you to the follow up question. That question is designed as a diffusing separation from the active offense of your presence and into the passive, departing from the present tense situation, and into a "maybe later" at the prospects convenience.

When developing this distinct and intuitive perception into the consumers response, you will know it happened when you have to ask yourself, was that it? When the consumer hesitates or thinks about a "yes" but answers "no," you should pick up on it. If you walk away asking if that was one then it probably was.

A thumbtack is a situation where an object or obstacle impedes a positive reading. A delivery package is the most common thumbtack. Often when I knock on the door, the person will peek out and look left and right as if expecting a package or mail. This means they are easily distracted even before I speak. If there is mail, junk mail, or even a delivery, the consumer will step out and the item will act as a deflection of attention and cross wires in my "truth detector" altering their response because their attention is not on answering your question but shared with the curiosity and concern for the object they are touching. This is the reason I do not leave a package or propaganda at the door or attempt to hand them anything. I want their attention to be 100% on my 8 second question and unprepared to respond with certainty. The more time they have to prepare a *"no"* even if it is a maybe, the less I will be able to read the results.

94

Throw in a thumbtack and my job is even more difficult to hear the undertone of the response.

Another Thumb tack would be a barking dog or a baby crying. I have had situations where the consumer is behind the door holding back a dog who will not stop barking. I cannot understand how a person would allow an animal to be so misbehaved. All I have to do is yell shut up to my dog, and he does. I have had many dogs and they get it. Yet I have had people come to the door with a small dog in their arms barking like mad while the handler tries to clamp their mouths to hear what I have to say. Sometimes I try to time my words between barks. It is a total fail in getting anywhere though. Even if I sense that they are interested, it's not like that damn dog will let me fulfill me next two objectives. I suppose I could ask them to come outside but that might be too much. Especially if the dog is that misbehaved I am sure it is a runner or even worse an ankle biter.

Another variety of thumbtack is the gardener or landscaper. I am not sure why the sound of a lawn mower or leaf blower gets my Irish up so much. If you are on a street where it seems like the gardeners are about to plug in their amps and start practicing their heavy metal music, I would recommend either you move away enough doors to not be blown out or even move to another street. I seriously feel like they are doing it on purpose.

There may be times when you are walking up to the door and see a pile of propaganda, maybe even your competition has left it. It is on a rare occasion that I will pick it up and place it conveniently on the porch like I am helping but moving it out of the line of sight from me to the consumer. Be careful though, if there is a camera or they walk out at the right time they may get mad. I have occasionally shoved it with a foot to the side and If it is my competition, I make sure that I step on it. Just kidding. Not.

The way to overcome a thumbtack is to listen carefully to the response of the individual. If you get any sign that they are not listening or that they are interested then ask the "maybe down the road" follow up question. Whether they say no, or yes, it does not hurt to try. Perhaps they were not listening and that if you rephrase or repeat the script you may break through.

"Without lead generation you have nothing. Without lead follow up you get nothing."- Me.

The ability to generate leads and prospects is the fun part. It feels like you are in control of your future. You can go out and go door to door and see results right away. If you have a bad day, you know that tomorrow is another day and that you can make up for it. It becomes addicting and very rewarding. Then when you get the lead, you must follow up with them because it is highly likely that unless you are in a business that you close at the door, you will have to follow up. You will have to type the name, number, email address and mailing address along with notes that help you as you build the relationship.

Have you heard of the funnel strategy? Imagine a funnel like the one you would use to fill your car oil tank. With the top area there is a large opening and at the bottom there is a small opening. The funnel strategy states you should look to fill as many leads into the large side of the funnel knowing that it will filter down and the most qualified leads make it to the bottom through the small hole. This suggests that the more leads you generate, the more you will have to qualify based on seriousness and urgency, and filter out the good from the bad because so many are bad. In sales we have 2 limitations. Time and space. I don't want to get metaphysical on you, but it's true. We have a limited amount of time to make the sale or we are out of the business. We also have a limited space that we must travel through to get to the customer to sign the contract. Sure you have digital signatures and email, but if you are like me, in real estate, you may need to visit the customer a few times as you build the relationship and travel times must be considered.

Having an effective system for capturing the contact and then have it set up to perform a "drip" campaign or a keep in contact campaign until the time of sale is everything. As of this writing, I am using several software applications and those may change so I will not name any today. I can describe the most important features of these applications to look for though.

The reason for tracking these efforts is that you can see your results and log your attempts at a sale. Also, having a software or app to tell you what happened today can help you when you return in a few months. For going door to door, having the ability to track me in real time via GPS is a must. I love the ability to watch myself on the map and tap on my location and have it accurately render the address of the current home. Some apps will require you to advance to the next home and force you to pay attention to the street address. This is one extra step I would rather not take. Door knocking is stressful enough, I need not be worried about whether I am putting in my notes onto the wrong person.

You should become quick at tapping on the screen and functioning as if the phone was a part of you. You will at first be very slow and clumsy. You will need to practice tapping on the screen in the right spot so that when you ask the prospect, *"would it be OK if I got your email address?"* you will not tap around, you will just be typing. Practice this a few times, trust me you will thank me on this. There is nothing worse than getting the lead and have to fudge your way around the phone while you are standing in front of them. Get fast and accurate as well. Be ready to switch applications if you find there are missing elements that would work better for your style of business. Me personally, I use very little functions inside of most applications because the more robust the door knocking app becomes the more I rely on managing 2 databases rather than taking the lead out of the door knocking app and putting the lead right into my preferred CRM on a desktop. That way I can do mailers, email, phone calls, You know, the 5 levels of marketing.

If your door to door application has the option to choose disposition, status, result or outcome and customize them, I suggest these. Program these statuses in order of frequency so they are handy and ready to tap. NOT HOME. This is even if someone answers the door but they are not the decision maker. NOT INTERESTED. This is when someone who "can" say yes, responds and it is a no. A decision maker who hears my pitch. RENTER. This may only matter if your business needs them to own the home. LEAD. A lead is a person who "can" say no, but they don't. This is a play on words but a very effective way of identifying a lead from a contact. A contact is a person who "can" say yes, but maybe they don't. DO NOT KNOCK or No soliciting, also people who are just plain rude or mean. I would rather never see them again. LEAD IN CRM. This is a status that I have found handy when knowing I have removed them from the door knocking app and put them into the desktop. Otherwise, I would not know if in fact I took them to the followup system. From there I have other statuses like RE-KNOCK. Often there will be people who become a lead at the door but then they never answer the phone and I know they are almost due. Just today I had one of those and they went with someone else because I did not knock again after several failed attempts at following up using the other four marketing methods and being ghosted.

The application I use can import and export data. This means I can grab a list of my leads in my CRM or perhaps a list of for sale by owners or expireds and map them for a knock campaign. I can import my hottest leads for a more targeted knocking session more like a GPS map to drive in what I call a *"target knock campaign."* This is when I stack a few hot leads that are "ghosting" me or need to see me today.

Chapter Six
What To Say and Do

"Why sell with blah-blah when you can sell with blah." -Floyd Wickman, Sales Trainer

I designed my script to have a sense of urgency and patience. I often get people who are almost perplexed that I am done with the questions and start walking away. I believe this is because they are used to being solicited by individuals who don't take no for an answer. I take no for an answer and so should you. However, you are also very aware that there are variations of no that sometimes have a maybe or even a yes undertone. Let me also preface the next pages by saying it was very hard to format the flow of the conversation and I would recommend you take these to flash cards. Since I am self publishing this beast, I could not figure out to indent without jacking up the whole page. It should make sense to you though…. I hope. I will put together a few of the most common scenarios. I just wish I could translate the minutia of body gestures involved in these responses because they are super precise. This precision is almost subliminal. I cover this as best I can in the chapter on body language and NLP. You could probably find the videos at JamesFestini.com. I cover this in my one on one and my door knock courses and seeing it is powerful.

I want to start you off with a typical scenario where the conversation flows in a most common manner where the prospect is less conversational and not a lead.

Agent: Hi My name is agent with company and I was wondering if you had any interest in selling your house?
Prospect: No.
Agent: Thank you very much, have a nice day. (That's it, nothing else walk away.)

Now for one where the prospect is mildly conversational and becomes a lead.

Agent: *Hi My name is agent with company and I was wondering i f you had any interest in selling your house?*
Prospect: Nah

Agent: Do you think maybe later down the road you would reconsider? Maybe (season?)

Prospect: Well my job, my wife, my aunt (whatever they say go to the next question)

Agent: *Do you have any idea where you'll be moving to?* (This is actually a shift in gears to displace the tension of getting the confession and back to friendly chatting.)

Prospect: No

Agent: *This City/State?* (Anyone who is serious would have clue. If
they were to tell you they don't know, then they might not be that go od of a lead.)

Prospect: Yes, next town

Agent: *So ideally when would you like to see a moving truck in your driveway?*

Prospect: Sooner or later (the answer to this question is only a ga uge for how motivated they might be.)

Although their answer is important,
it does not change the next question.

Agent*: Great, do you have any idea how much the value of the ho me might be?*

Prospect: No (the same as yes I check online etc.)

Agent: *It's my job to know the prices in this neighborhood and if you don't mind I would like to keep you updated on the current mark et conditions. It's no problem, can I get your email address that way when you are ready we can talk. What is a good email
address?* (Assume they will give it and look at your phone to type it)

Prospect: I don't have or want to give.

Agent: *No Problem, Do you mind if I keep in touch every
once in a while maybe later we can talk?*

Prospect: Yes.

Agent: *Can I get your number so I can call instead of just
popping by? (*You must then look at your phone and assume they are about to give it to you. You also need to start the number by calling out the area code. For example, I say *"714"* with a pause and they cannot help but finish the sentence.

Prospect: No

Agent: *OK, here's my*
card,call me if you ever need my help. Thank you very much and hav
e a nice day.

Here is a scenario where the prospect is a complete jerk.

Agent: *Hi My name is agent with company and I was wondering i
f you had any interest in selling your house?*
Prospect: Any angry thing. Let your worst fear and imagination
roll as you get penetrated by their miserable attitude and likely
miserable life.

Agent: *I am sorry to bother you. Thank you and have a nice day.*
Step away slowly and look like a dog that just got kicked and
show them you are a pathetic wimp. No joke. Any sign of
confrontation or resistance will light their fire. On rare occasions,
that jerk may be your next client, but that is rare. See the chapter on
dealing with angry people

The Close: *Actually, I would like to come back out to the house
and see what you have and crunch some numbers. That way you
have a better idea of what direction to take. What's your schedule
like? Today at 5 or would tomorrow at 6 be better?* Always use
alternate times so they choose between two one instead of saying no
to one.

Prospect: Well, I am not ready for that.
Agent: *OK, here's my*
card, please call me if you ever need my help. Thank you very much
and have a nice day.

Like I said, these variations in responses will flow almost the
same but it is up to you which one you pull out and for who. The
words are precise and you must also be precise in pronunciation and
delivery. Just because you have said it hundreds of times does not
mean you can slur or mumble. Be well spoken and they will respect
this.

"Keep your words impeccable".- Don Miguel Ruiz.

When you get to the door, I expect that you will get objections. The funny thing is that you will get the same objections that you would get on the phones and there are only three kinds of objections. Yes, maybe or no. Let's handle a few of them. There are so many objections you can get so study and memorize everyone you can. I never say my objection handlers are original or the best but I claim that my introduction and approach to initial contact is the best.

Let's start with the most obvious.

"No."
This is a no brainier. But it is VERY important that you listen to how they say no. Are they a definite no or are they a reluctant no? My theory is that it is almost impossible to say no if they have yes on their mind. Even the hardest sellers cannot lie to me because I have practiced the art of listening. If you listen to the response, you find that sometimes the owner will say no with their mouth, but they will say yes with their body and tone. I would say one of my greatest assets is the skill I have gained from hearing the word no hundreds of thousands if not millions of times and training my ear to hear when no means maybe. If you sense that this is in fact a definitive "no" then you can respond with…

"Well, thank you very much. Have a nice day."

"Nah"
This differs from a NO. This is a reluctant answer of a homeowner who is caught off guard. We must deliver the next follow up question with an innocent, almost Columbo style.

"Do you think maybe later down the road you would reconsider?"
This will either continue as a reluctant no or a become certain no. If it is a solid no, then you should still ask the diversion follow up question below, but normally I just say thank you have a nice day and leave. The diversion laced follow up question is..

"Do you have any idea what the house is worth?"

There is also a bit of body language that has me looking at the roof lines and areas to suggest like I am lending an expert eye and that this might subliminally make them feel curious to get this insight from me. That is if they even care. If they care they open up and if they don't they don't open up.

The reason I call this a diversion is that this question is more of a conversational over a confrontational question that would be more chit chat than interrogation that would have the prospect feeling defensive. Regardless of whether they say yes or no it's my goal to share my opinion via email. I do this with a casual request like this.

"Would it be OK if I could email you some information on the market values, Maybe later down the road, if the numbers look good you might call me?" Again there is a body language that can only be described like a *"please don't hit me for asking this question but if you give it to me I will totally be thankful."*

What if they say *"It's not a good time,"* or *"it's a bad time?"*
This is a judgment call. Only you can make this call how bad of a time is it. Because the script is fast, you can say something like, *"Sorry, I was just wondering if you were thinking of selling your house."* It is likely that you already did the intro and they say *"bad time"* just a few words in. If they say anything other than *"no"* you again make the call. Can you ask, *"Can I come back tomorrow for a quick chat?"* If they say, *"no"* then it's no. There will be times where they might say yes but it's not a good time and they close the door.

What if they say *yes or not right now* and slam the door?
Now we have a dilemma. Are they messing with you or are they selling soon? The only way to respond is to obviously leave your propaganda and come back the next day. At that time, you knock and say, *"Hi, my name is agent and I came by yesterday and it seemed like a bad time, but you made it sound like you might be considering selling your home soon. Are you?"*

This will go 2 ways. They are going to hate that you came back, and you will have to be great at recovery and rapport or they may engage in conversation. There may be a third option. The person at the door is different. In this case it a new pitch with a careful listen. I sense that it is likely that they will probably sell but not with you and that is why they slammed the door. Which leads me to the next situation.

What if they say *yes but we have an agent?*

Tricky indeed. This a slippery slope to get on. You first must determine the relationship with this agent. Is the agent their blood relative or is it the agent that leaves notepads at the door every quarter and they never met them. Your question must be delicately injected.

You will ask. *"Just out of curiosity how did you choose the agent that will sell the home?"*

When you hear the answer, you will know how to handle it. If they say that it is their mom, then you might not get the deal. You could proceed with that and ask if they are local where they work. Sometimes the second answer will reveal a smoke screen. They could say that mom is a retired agent and she knows of a friend at the office or some B.S. If this is the case then you may have a chance for a referral to the agent and you step in. If it is the local agent that they may or may not know their name, then you might be able to double back with a delivery of a presentation package or product demo.

It not what you say, but how you say it. Yeah, Right. It is what you say and how you say it. I could write another book on the ways to engage a prospect and convert them into a sale. The only thing I can close this chapter with is that if they are not interested, you will not sell them. Some say that is wrong but I am not here for converting those who are not interested. I am looking for those who are not ready yet. So many times I have played the hardcore closer game only to have the prospect cancel the contract after a few days or weeks. I want clients who will stick with me until I get paid. If I do a good job, they will refer me. Find a script that works for you. Memorize every script and objection. Internalize and make a part of your DNA, and practice hearing the variations of no and yes that might come your way. That way when you get hit with an objection, instinct will deliver the perfect response. Do not just have one way of answering a rebuttal. Have 5 and have a choice for which one you feel will work best right here right now.

You will often find individuals that are not ready to transact during the holidays or the winter. However, they are telling you they are totally motivated to do this after the new year. I love door knocking during the winter. Everybody is in a much nicer mood, granted they are in more of a hurry and do not want to talk about the future after Christmas and New Year's sometimes. The weather is so much better for going the distance. Besides you are probably eating way too much junk in November and December so this is only a bonus to walk it off. Also, the air is crisp . I have a perfect temperature to go the distance. It is about 55-75 with a light breeze and maybe a cloud or two. I live in Southern California so this is pretty much from November to February. I know you are jealous. Until you see our taxes, traffic, cost of living, fires and occasional earthquake and mudslides, but hey, it's all good. I have prepared a few good answers to the objections for these winter wavering suspects that might land you a contract sooner rather than later. Change these as you see fit. It is better if you memorize and internalize them so that when you wing it you wing it with confidence.

I think the home would look better in the spring/summer
Perhaps, with some green grass and fresh roses blooming. However, the holidays have so much emotion tied to memories of home for the holidays. Buyers get to see the area with all the decorations and get a feel of the holiday cheer.

One reason buyers pay top dollar is because they make a purchase based on emotion. They will probably drive the neighborhood at night too and love the lights and decorations in the area. They will get a feeling that this is a great community. Getting an emotional buyer motivated to buy your home for top dollar because they love it instead of liking it would be better for you right? I also love the way the photos turn out with winter lighting. I can get a photographer in here by Friday, will that work for you?

Nobody is buying homes during the holiday, or there are fewer buyers during the holidays.
You are right, Mr. Name, there are fewer homes sold during the winter/holiday. Historically, I have sold more homes during the last

3 months of the year than in the summer. The winter/holiday buyers are more serious about buying a home. It's not like people go out cruising open houses because the weather is great. This means that only serious buyers are out shopping. You want the serious buyers only right?

You already said you did not want lookie-loos or open house nosy neighbors and you want every buyer to be pre-qualified. By having the home on the market during the holidays, this almost guarantees a higher percentage of ready to buy house hunters. Also, there will be fewer homes on the market to compete with and you know about supply and demand right? If you are the only one in the area for sale, you create the demand. Right now the inventory is low and the interest rates are also low. This market compared to the market in the spring might be better for you wouldn't you agree?

I don't want to move during the winter/holidays.
That is OK because you probably won't be moving during the holidays. It takes about a month to close an escrow once we find a buyer. And in the area I am seeing about a month to 2 months depending on price for that to happen. So worst/best-case scenario is you are moving in the first week of January or as late as February.

If we can time it so that when you are packing up the decorations you are also packing up the house, you can tackle two messes at once. This way you can enjoy the holidays with the family, we can always put the home on a temporary no show for any dinners or parties and then right after the holidays you can start packing. To be honest, though I have had buyers want to see a home on Christmas Eve because that was their only day off. Fortunately, that home was vacant, and that home sold. I'm not saying this will happen but hey if you get someone that hot, you never know. Let's try it.

This may be the longest chapter because after so many doors I have really put a lot of thought into each outcome and how to best handle yourself while at the doors. These are the "what if" variables of door knocking.

You are dressed to the nines and have your propaganda. Your hygiene is on point and you are ready to make contact. You are walking up to the door and no one answers. You walk away and see a car pulling into the driveway. What do you do? I will cover these and many other scenarios in this section. Again, these are situations that you may not even give much thought to but lucky for you I have. It would surprise you how these varied situations are common but that they are specific to engagement with successful outcomes.

Lets say you are at the door and the garage door opens. Step back quick. About 10 feet away. This is very scary when someone opens the door and there is a stranger standing there. If you can even make it appear as if you just came off the street and not be already standing there, that's even better. Maybe pace back a few steps and spin around again like you almost forgot to stop. I know it sounds strange, but these body signals are to put people at ease in what could be a startling situation. Especially if you are a large man and the person opening the door is a little old lady who lives alone and clutches her purse like she's holding the crown jewels. As you engage, step slowly and with a reluctant, non aggressive demeanor as you ask the question. If they seem inviting, you can move closer because they will at some point need to hear you which about 7 feet. I talk about this space in the chapter on personal space and body language.

Here is another variation of a common probability. The driver pulls into the driveway and you are standing at the door. Turn back around smile and wave. Not a long creepy smile and weird wave but a small "what's up" familiar greeting. Sometimes the individual will be on the phone in the car or be taking a few moments to gather their belongings. Maybe there is a kid in the car or groceries. Whatever world they are in you are not part of it so you must be quick and concise. As they step out of the car, you must assess their urgency and their state of mind. You should play out each scenario with what they might look at is the defensible space. A mother taking out a child is about 15 feet away for a man and 7 for a woman salesperson. A little lady with a cane and a hearing aide is about 10 feet. A massive man with a sledgehammer after his cross fit gym trip is about 7 feet.

You need to recognize the clues right away, about what is the situation that the homeowner just arrived from and where they are going. That way you can assess the timing and delivery of your script according to them being caught off guard and busy. This may be one of those moments that you can see what they were doing just before you arrived and what they are about to do. A mom with four kids in sports uniforms at 7 at night, the kids' uniforms are dirty, tells me they are coming back from sport. Whereas a clean uniform at 4 pm screams we are late to sport and I may not have time to pitch. Unless you are Sheldon " The Machine" Levine, in that case you offer to go to the game.

Are they on the phone? Does it look like they are wrapping up the call? Will they be there for a bit? I just stand there for a few of seconds before I get the point. They will not engage. I would just walk away. Tag that they are home and when you go back by, knock on that door. If they step out of the car, be at hearing distance, about 10 feet or five steps, so they are not frightened by your presence but comfortable with your just standing there. When they get out or sometimes, they will just roll down their window, because you are scary, ask your question. Just like at the door. Thank them and walk away. Another valid reason for leaving the propaganda with the stealth drop. Otherwise, you will be forced to hand them something they don't want or need as they carry a baby or bags.

This is kind of the same suggestion if they are mowing the lawn or using a power tool. This differs from whether they are using a chainsaw or a shovel. If they have to turn off tools, then you might have to judge for each one. If I walk up to the a man and a lawn mower and they look like they on the last row and almost done, then I will walk slow. If they are in the middle of something such as putting up roof tiles, Christmas lights, or drilling into an eave at 20 feet in the air, I might wait a minute but not look like I am waiting right in front of them. Sometimes they are in the garage but they are on a ladder in the attic. I wait or I walk away. These situations are ideal for the use of an app to mark as not home and just remember them for when you double back on the other side of the street. I would still stealth drop in case I don't make it back.

I almost went into a whole thing about dogs and realized that I wrote a chapter called what if there is a dog? I suppose dealing with a second soul is why I had to do a whole chapter. Perhaps it is because it is like dealing with a family member and just like a renter or sibling they have a mind of their own and thus requires some scripts and steps to handle them.

What if there is a gated community? I would assume that if this is the case, they might not allow you to knock. Often they will have a sign at the gate stating this. I do not care if you live there. That might be worse. However, I would think leaving your propaganda might be a gray area.

What if the cops stop you? I have had this happen. A homeowner saw a suspicious person going door to door. I am sure they even said looking in the windows and trying to open doors. Read this ridiculousness in my chapter on the ring doorbell and cameras. This will be an advantage that you are professionally dressed and composed. A nightclub pimp or a hooker is not professional and will land you in cuffs in some areas. Remember, you are doing dozens of presentations. Your job is to be neutral and pleasurable with no judgment. When a cop pulls up next to you what will they assume? That they should search you for drugs or weapons or let you go because that neighbor is just a busybody? I am serious about this. We all judge. Don't stand before the judge with your personality on your sleeve. Let your words speak for you.

What if they find your propaganda as you walk away or even call you later to complain about leaving it behind? If they walk out to talk, and they often do. Sometimes the prospect will see your marketing piece on the ground. I say in a "oh by the way" tone, *"oh, yeah I leave that just in case you don't answer. It's information on X"* and then break back into conversation. Assuming that they will not hand it back. If you gesture as if you will take it, trust me, they will give it back. That is not the goal. Let them throw it out. I have had people call and leave a voice mail saying that I should not litter. I once had someone yell "pick that up!" from a window. I could not see who it was, and it sounded like teenager messing with me. So I stopped in my tracks, looked around and then I picked it up. Then I carried it closer to the door and put it down again. I typed a whole slew of scenarios of confrontations below and then moved it to the chapter on dealing with angry people.

Do Not Knock List. I never heard of such a thing until I moved to Yorba Linda. There was an ordinance passed in the city after a few issues with break-ins. I am certain that many of those registered do not even recall being on it. I had to register with the city and even get fingerprinted with the police. I did their dance and was registered. Fortunately, the city keeps a log of the registrations on a file. I could get that list on a digital file and got it into my door knocking app. Now as I approach the door, I can see who is on that list.

If there is a "No Soliciting" sign. Don't knock. I am sure there are different interpretations for this little sign. I feel that it is OK to leave my propaganda at the doorstep but not knock. Some may say that it is a solicitation. It's your call. Even if I had someone call me to define it with a complaint, which I have not yet, I will continue to deliver the goods. Now there are those who have a sign on the door that reads "No soliciting, we do not need solar, we have found God, and we don't want any cookies." They might have the one that reads no fliers or pamphlets. This one I will leave nothing. I don't know why people ask If I knock when I post my photo collection of new and unusual no soliciting signs on social media. Unless the house is on fire or there is a mandatory evacuation and you are a cop or firefighter, do not mess around.

What if you don't see the sign until you knock? I have been here. I walk up and the sign is old and faded or in a spot that I would not see unless I went looking for it. When the owner gets to the door, I break into my script and just at the end, kind of like I just saw it, will then glance and stare with a "duh" look and say I am sorry I did not even see the sign. Sorry to bother you. This is a second by second play out though. Often you might get all the way through with no resistance. Sometimes they will say,"can't you read you dummy?" Again apologize and thank them. Oh, and grab your propaganda on the way out as long as they cannot see you do this, like if it is around the front of the garage out of the line of site. I do not want them closing the door and fuming only to walk out later and think I did the stealth drop after they chewed me out in an act of vengeful litter.

If there is a mailbox. I am not a lawyer but from what I gather, do not touch the mailbox. It can be considered tampering, even though you own the box, it is also owned by the feds. U.S. Code Title 18 section 1725, says it is illegal. Even on the outside. I don't even put it on one of those large columns with elaborate brickwork and perfect shelf for your propaganda.

If you get to the door and they say they are renting. I would ask them this question. "Have you thought about buying in this area?" You might pick up a buyer. Sometimes they might mention that the owner will sell or that they are moving out. The odds of you getting the strangers to give up the landlord's number are rare. I suppose you could ask but it's not likely. Even if they give it to you there is a high probability that the number is on the do not call list and as you all might know, I comply with this law. It is NOT a federal do not call "suggestion," it is a law and I am not into breaking the rules. Oh, I am sure that you have some excuses or logic behind being able to "get around" the rule. Perhaps your other guru told you to use a script that avoids the solicitation. Unless you are looking to rent the home or have a renter ready to move in this is a total lie. If it's true, then give your renter prospect the number. Getting around the law is the same thing as breaking it. It's the same thing as a white lie. This is like having a drink is not drinking. If you can get the number, like I do through asking or searching online directories, or just putting it into my CRM, which is very complete, there you can bounce it against the do not call list.

Sometimes you will get to a door and the sun will be hitting the occupant in the face when they open. I try to knock on the side of the street where I will be shaded and the sun will be timed better for my arrival. Just be aware that if this is unavoidable you may have to step to the side where you do not look like The Messiah coming from the sky as a shadow in the light.

What if they are having a party? This depends. I have walked past a small group standing in the driveway and depending on my comfort and gut level that day I might approach and ask. Maybe only four or five people because you have a hard time identifying the owner. You kind of have to just look at one and hope it is the one. It's a crap shoot. Often the other party is right next door and will volunteer that they are not either. I have occasionally had one point to the other and say "I am not but they are." Sometimes in jest but then I just ask, *"no, seriously?"* In that situation sometimes the individual will step forward and I can have that quick, and I mean quick, chat. So quick that I just say something like, *"now might not be a good time but can I get your number and call you tomorrow? Oh, and your email so I can send you my info?"* Always get their email.

Let's suppose the party is inside and there are balloons and jumpers. I would just walk past. I am not good with interrupting adults with their kids at a party and the kids will be the biggest thumbtack. However, if you sense that the party is wrapping up, and the owner is outside, this may be a judgment call. Determine if you are interrupting or not. You will not have a valuable conversation with a mother carrying bags and cake. Never help carry groceries in the house, this is out of line and maybe very creepy. Unless you are well known in the area and they remember you from other visits.

What if the party is inside and they a bunch of Golden Girls playing bridge? Then I would knock. As for windows, don't be a peeping Tom. If you see people in the window, do not make eye contact and really try to avoid all gazes in that directing. Just remain oblivious to the fact that they live their life in a fishbowl. If they go to the window or wave you on, then smile wave and walk away. Leaving your propaganda that you already left.

I hate to confess that I have tripped and broke a sprinkler or two. I have broken no other decoration or water features. If you do this, assume that you are on camera. Just as you would leave a note on a car you hit in a parking lot, leave a note, or at least you should.

Sometimes I see a newspaper on the driveway and I will pick up up and walk it to the door as a good deed. I won't hold it and hand it to them, but I will also attempt to put it out of line of sight so as not deliberately create a thumbtack if they start to read the paper instead of reading me. It is your call to do this or not. What if they like to pick up the paper from the driveway and never go to the door and then you got the paperboy in trouble? Whatever. Do not touch any packages or mail and as for other agents propaganda I am tempted to kick it or step on it but this would look bad on camera.

Sometimes you might walk across a home that has a fruit tree or avocado tree. You think to yourself; I am hungry and pull one. This is stealing. Now if you are on a sidewalk and there is a massive fruit tree overhanging from a block wall fence and it is safe to assume everyone grabs these, you are still on shaky ground. This is your call. I often see kumquats. These are tiny little orange like fruits that grow by the hundreds on mature trees. I am guilty of nabbing one or two in the past cause they are simple to pop in your mouth and go. This compared to grabbing a pomegranate, orange, grapefruit or avocado is logistically different. If I see a tree in a pot with 10 little ones all alone, I will not touch that one. It is probably wrong either way but I think the person with the massive tree is probably happier to get rid of them versus the one who is proud of the little tree and rubs all 10 weekly in anticipation of their birth.

The same thing goes for flowers and roses. These I never touch. I photograph them if I am inspired. Paying careful attention to the camera angle and I make a thumbs up gesture to nobody in particular just in case I am being watched. I imagine a homeowner would be cool with a photo at the right angle that is not taking a picture of their house but of a plant that they know is cool. The opposite being taking a picture of the front of their home because the roses look good at that angle. Just skip it. Always assume you are being watched or on camera.

Do not walk on a lawn, ever, even if the lawn is dead. Even if the lawn is rocks and weeds. It is a sign of laziness and disrespect. If the home has a front lawn that is pure concrete this is not a lawn it is a driveway and fine. Do not hop bushes unless you land in cement. Like for example, if there is a very low hedge or gap in between two homes that is only a separator from one driveway to the other than that might be OK. Depending on the architecture and position of the home you may leap right into an open garage door and startle someone or even a dog. Damn dogs.

What if a kid answers the door? This is awkward. I have had kids looking like they are less than 3 years old opening the door. I step back and smile and ask if your mom or dad are home? Sometimes the parents rush to the door totally startled and depending on your appearance and distance they will assume pervert or peddler. Read my chapter on body language to work on this. If the kid stands there too long, I just have to walk away. A child from the ages of 1-13, I would ask if their mom or dad are home. If they say, *"no"* I just say, *"thank you or never mind,"* and walk away… fast. The rudest people in the world are boys between the age of 14-17. I don't know what they have been watching on the screen to make them so rude, but it is real. They are the ones who say something nasty or close the door as they look at you like they farted left you to smell it. Again, you just thank them with a have a nice day and walk away. If the kid is holding a dog make it quick cause kids suck at holding back dogs. If you walk up and the family is playing with their kids, I would make that judgment call. If dad is teaching the kids to ride a bike, I might stop and smile with a face of my own fond memories. Most of the time I might pass on this one because I don't want to ruin a moment.

Every one of these what if moments require asking this question. Is it a bad time and will I make it worse by engaging them? Let us assume it will always be a bad time. Now all we have to do is decide if you can lessen the damage to their personal time by asking them a question that for my industry is maybe 1 out of 100 people who will actually not be bothered by the irrelevant question I have to ask.

"I always feel like somebody's watching me" -Rockwell

Just assume there are cameras everywhere. I thought that was enough for this chapter, but that would be too easy. There are so many places to be seen as you go door to door and oftentimes you may never even see them. If you do not have a doorbell with a camera, I would suggest you get one. They are great. If you have one I would assume it is the most popular kind that goes by the name of Ring. I'm telling you this brand is at about one out of every five doors I approach. The inventor started on his own and then Amazon bought it. Must be nice. I own one of these and I understand what happens when an object passes by. Depending on the position and angle of the camera, you could be triggering a recording and even and alarm from the sidewalk. Inside of this camera is a very high definition lens with a very wide angle. It also has a sound and auto recording. The camera is connected to an app on the users smart phone and it plays in real time. Let me describe how to handle these.

As you are approaching the front door, the user/owner has two alarms that get triggered. The user also has the option to set up parameters and zones that would trigger these alarms on their phone. One alarm is a proximity warning, and the other is a doorbell ring. So even if you do not ring the doorbell you can be sure the resident knows you have arrived. This alarm drives me crazy at home because my wife has her app to trigger anyone who walks past the front of the home and it goes off all the time. Perhaps you are one of these people.

As you are walking up to the door and assuming that you are always on camera, even if it it not a Ring you must behave yourself. I have probably been recorded adjusting myself, if you know what I mean, or maybe just walking like a bum instead of someone who exudes confidence. There is a lot you can say with your posture and body language with your walk. Especially a smile. I see cameras mounted inside of windows and I see them on the eaves of the home in front of me and even behind me as I turn and walk away. So if you need to scratch your butt, I suggest you do this on the sidewalk because you are less likely to be seen there.

When you approach a home and see that there is a camera doorbell, I recommend you ring it and take a step back. I also recommend that you always knock. Unless you hear a doorbell, like to hear it in the home, not from the device, you cannot be sure they heard it on the phone app. That is one problem with these doorbells. If the owner has their phone off or on do not disturb they will not hear it. So always, always knock, unless it is an old-fashioned doorbell and when you ring it you hear the chime inside.

The camera on this device is usually a fish eye lens at about 3-4 feet high. A fish eye lens has a wide angle effect the bulges the viewers image kind of like those cute puppy photos you see where their faces are distorted to make their nose look huge. This means you have to adjust you body to speak into it because you are probably talking to them face to face in a distorted zoom. The center of the lens is the center of their best view. Do not just lean in like you are talking to a speaker and put your junk and belly in their face.

Another flaw in this device is that the signal is often horrible. You may hear someone answer but it could be totally broken up. If you sense that this is the case you must speak clearly and you may even have to repeat or even cut the script into Morse code down to *"you want to sell your house?"* Either way, speak with a clear tone and a normal volume at the camera. The microphone on these are super sensitive so there is no need to move in too far.

This is the scenario as it often happens. You are walking up the door and the resident hears a chime on their phone. You press the doorbell once and hear the familiar chime. You take a 5 foot distance from the door, likely about 4 feet from the doorbell. This puts you in a full body view from the door and for the camera. DO NOT look into the camera yet and for the love of Pete do not wave at cameras before you are engaged. Unless there is a sign that says smile you are on camera. But even then don't go looking for this. It's creepy. You may or may not hear the device pick up. If they are in a loud place then you will hear their background noise. Pay attention to if they are driving and assuming they are busy so make is clean and fast. You will hear a "hello?" If it clear then you need to know you are being looked at. The way the app works is that the conversation happens on the smart phone with a view of the door and a two-way conversation. Unlike a walkie talkie or intercom, this requires no extra buttons. You then squat or crouch with your torso as upright as you can and centered about 4 feet from the camera like you are in a photo booth and deliver the script.

There will be times when you are talking to the camera and someone will also come to the door. Depending on where you are in the conversation you can address the person in front of you with this script. *"I was just talking to your wall."* I use this as a joke and sometimes they laugh. Then I just jump into the script all over again. You will need to use logic in this case. If the husband is on the doorbell and it is very clear, he said no, it would not make sense to start over with the wife as he listens. He will be part of the conversation all over again and this is awkward. Change the script a bit and say, *"I am an agent with company and I was just asking* (vs. wondering because that identifies the existing conversation) i*f you were thinking of selling your house?"* The real estate script is super short anyhow so we can deliver it in its entirety. Other industries may have to redeliver the pitch and almost completely ignore that guy on the doorbell because they will not get you anywhere.

There is a variation of this approach without a camera but with a speaker and a microphone or an intercom device. There is actually a device that is in a light fixture with and without a camera. I am not sure how the tech behaves on this one as far as the user interface but let's assume it is similar. The ones I have ran into have an incredible sound quality. One time I was standing at the door and no one answered and as I walked away someone said, "hello?" I swear to you I jumped because it sounded as if they were standing right there. You will always be able to tell if there is a camera by a glass bulb bulging out. Often if it a small plastic square it is just a motion sensor or light sensor. It is not common to manufacture cameras with plastic covers because the lenses fade and scratch.

I have often wondered if it is worthwhile to walk up to the doorbell and ring it and if no one answers then you just bust into a script to nobody on the other side. It is recording and this would be the equivalent of leaving a voice mail on an answering machine or a video email. The only downside is that what if they are watching and just not answering. That would be weird… unless they reply. Then I suppose it is good. What if they did not set to record? This is probably not the case, but you may be talking to a wall. Test this out for yourself if you have a device and get a feel for the interaction and what the flow would look like.

Pay attention to whether or not their lens is dirty or directed at the sun. This may be a problem because they cannot see you very well. The OCD camera guy side of me wants so badly to clean the lens, but that could be perceived as tampering instead of helping. What I do is if I see a dirty lens as I am about to touch the bell I will run my finger along the lens super casual and discreet. This is assuming that my finger is not greasy or dirty and would make it worse. I hate to see a lens with a layer of crud blocking the view. As a side rant, have you ever seen someone with dirty glasses and wonder how the hell do they not see that? Then you think well they probably can't and that is why they have glasses. But wait, would it still make a huge difference? I was always cleaning my moms super thick Coke-bottle glasses because I swear they looked like she used them to stir chicken soup.

If you are subscribed to the local Ring social media pages online where residents post videos of "porch pirates" being recorded by cameras, you would laugh at the comments. There was one that showed a man putting his propaganda on the door and yet the posting says to be aware of this man trying to open doors. The comments were hilarious after. Another one was of a person stealing a package and as they jumped off the porch, they broke their leg and the partner had to help them walk away. Even funnier is this inventor that builds devices that are triggers to record thieves who grab a package with a bobby trap. With the camera linked to a GPS tracker and a video signal to relay the recording they would have the box recording the thief putting it in their car and taking it home and then opening it. The funny part is that they make a wheel with a fan to be triggered at the opening to explode in a super fine confetti of powder that is super hard to clean up and then triggers a fart spray along with police chatter suggesting that the package is being tracked. The reactions are awesome and he should get a job at Amazon developing similar tech.

Needles to say you must assume you are always being recorded and watched. Do not walk on lawns, do not touch car windows to place your flier, look around to see that your stealth drop is not being filmed, avoid opening doors or gates that might be seen as prowler behavior.

Sometimes you will see a cool decoration or a sign that you want to photograph. I have a large collection of clever "No Soliciting" signs online. When I do this, I will make it very fast and afterwords, assuming I am on film or being watched, I will gesture with thumbs up or and an exaggerated smile or laugh out loud to show my excitement about such a cool item. That way if they see me they can read my body language is not of someone gathering reconnaissance and casing the joint but in fact enamored with their style and taste. I would never take a photo of the whole house unless they decorate it with something so unique that the owner would know why you did this such as Halloween or Christmas. I often will photograph cool water features or beautiful plants or landscaping or lawn decor. I am waiting for the day that someone posts something about a large black man scoping out houses with a large handgun at his side. I dress in all black and my messenger bag is likely seen as a bulge on cameras that could be seen as a weapon. A very large one, but hey, people have active imaginations. Again, go to the social feeds of these doorbell groups and you will see the conspiracy theories fly. This is also why you dress professionally. Wearing nice apparel with a large recognizable logo is always better.

I hate dogs and door knocking. It's not that I don't like dogs, I just hate them when I have to meet them on their turf under what they consider to be threats to the owners according to the dog. I have always had a dog. I hope you dog lovers don't get all poopy because I said this. Forgive me. I am just convinced that all dogs want to eat me. It only took getting bit by two dogs for them to know that James Festini is scared. My bites were minor and not during the knocks, but now all dogs sense it.

Much of my fears of having a dog eat me or run away is made easier to deal with by knowing the approach. You should read the chapter on The Approach. Basically, there are telltale signs that show if there is a dog on the premises. A bloody leg bone of a large cow is one. A pile of dog poop is another. Some chewed up dog toys or a bowl of water. Perhaps a leash or a sign that says beware of dog. That's a good one. Sometimes I feel like there is an attack dog on a 72-hour fast and I am their re-feed so I will just skip that. No door left behind I know but I also say no body parts left behind either.

What if a dog comes charging at the screen door and slams into it but it does not open yet continues to bark loud and hard as if to hunger for your bloody arm? Calmly stabilize your heart attack and stand your ground and wait for the owner to come to the door to tell their vicious dog to shut up and let you ask your question. Sometimes, I apologize for the interruption. I have had a homeowners injure their dog trying to shut them up. I did not see it, but I heard from behind the door a persons voice and then a yelp like maybe they stepped on it. I just say an innocent but polite I'm sorry and go right into my script.

Sometimes you will walk up to the door and there is a homeowner in the garage working on their car and their dog is sitting nearby. As I pass, they will stand up and bark or just approach me. It's right around that time that the homeowner yells at me to say he does not bite, or he yells at the dog to come back. Many times, the dog does not listen and ends up either rubbing up against me or just sniffing me. Sometimes they hop onto my leg and put a little dirt on it. Even then I apologize for the interruption and get to the script. But don't make a habit of saying I'm sorry each time you knock. Instead, say it in your tone and body language. I have heard that communication is 80% body language and tone and 20% what you say. If that's the case, use this as leverage.

What if the dog is barking so loud and does not shut up and yet the homeowner looks at you like you will get your message out? Like they can somehow hear and understand what you say over the completely out-of-control dog, just say your words. They may say maybe and then you are forced to chat. By that time the owner will probably come outside closing the door and leaving the dog inside. At this point just make it quick. Especially if the dog is still going nuts. Trying to time you words in between barks is difficult, but I have tried that too.

What if a dog comes charging out as you come to the door? Yeah, I really don't have an answer that is the right one. I stand still and say a little prayer. Depending on the breed, this prayer might also be accompanied by my life flashing before my eyes and crapping a little. I have never been attacked, but I am prepared for it. I have grown up with dogs and I know to handle them. In play I have learned to wrestle with them without getting bit. But then again, my dogs did not really want me dead so maybe they made it easy. In California you can carry pepper pray for self-defense. I run in the streets with pepper spray. Not for a human attack but for dogs. I don't know the laws on trespassing and "Macing" a family pet and I don't want to know. Some states do not allow the sale of pepper spray. I recommend a brand called Sabre 3 in 1 runner pepper spray with adjustable hand strap. It is small and discreet. I can hold my cell phone and the device in the palm of my hand.

I am also prepared if the dog makes it past my spray. I know that the dog will go for my limbs or my face. I will protect the face at all costs. I may have to sacrifice my forearm for them to chew on until the owner stops the animal. I will deal with the legalities later. Gruesome, I know. But it is better to be ready than to be mauled by a dog ending your door knocking either by the insecurity or the massive scars on your face or the scars of the attack that you will never go out again.

You should also check on the laws for your state regarding trespassing. If a sign saying no trespassing is posted and you walk on the land and the dog attacks, you may have a problem. I am not looking to sue or get sued in my life ever. If a dog bites me and I have to pay a doctor, then there may be a legal action. I am not a lawyer but I understand that dog owners have a responsibility even on private land to make sure that a dog will not attack. I hate this topic. Be careful my friends and be ready and watchful.

What if the dog runs through the doors and runs away? Then try to help. Often this just makes the dog run. The homeowner will have to come out half naked and maybe even walk into the street. I have seen this. You are there standing for a few awkward moments trying to offer a stranger help because it is all your fault. Sometimes the owner is mad and sometimes they are not. I blame the owner 99% in my head because I think "how long have you had this dog and you still don't know how to open the door without it running away or trained it not to?'

I have had dogs, and they were always in the backyard but I am sure my dogs hear me deliver one growling sit or stay with very little training and they do just that. Still, it is super awkward when they say don't worry and the pitch is over and you walk to the next door and the next and still see that owner wrangling up the dog. Even worse is the dog sets off all the area dogs to start barking in a K9 concerto titled A-hole Salesperson Coming to Your Door Number 5. I touch on one of these stories in my "Dealing With Angry People" chapter. I have also had one where the owner has to go back inside and get in his car because that dog was fast and they were old. Too old to be dealing with the crap I just dealt them. What a jerk I am. Next door.

I was wrapping up the book for publishing and the very next day my daughter became a Girl Scout, the week of their cookie season. The moment I heard about my kid having to sell something, my brain went into overdrive. I almost wanted to go before the Girl Scout world and take the stage at their next sales summit. Assuming they have one. I wonder if they even hire world class sales trainers to write their scripts and do workshops? See what I mean? I am fired up over this one. So much so that this chapter is for the ladies. Especially the little ladies.

There is no doubt in my mind that selling anything door to door is hard. The female of our species has a tremendous advantage and a huge disadvantage at the same time. The disadvantage is safety.

Ladies, be safe.

If something does not feel right, do not go in a strangers home. Make sure you are accounted for every second. Even if you have to find a friend or relative to go on face time as you knock for two hours then do this. It would be a great excuse to talk to mom. Their advantage is they are the symbol of trust and innocence. As a woman in this era you can be trusted and respected. If you are professional, in appearance and well spoken, you will go very far. The men have to deal with the stigma of the crooked salesperson going door to door selling vacuum cleaners.

Let me talk about my favorite salesperson of them all. The Girl Scouts of America. I know other countries have their version of these little characters who learn entrepreneurship and team building through challenges. My little girl is turning eight this week and we have a lot of scripts to cover. I will share with you her training and marketing plan as I have manifested it.

First, we will create a 60 second video introducing her and the cookies. I have good video skills so this will turn out amazing. Next we will post it on every social platform that we know. We will print out fliers with QR codes that will link to the online site for those who are not home. If I had more time, I would rip DVDs of the movie and leave those at the doors too. I have hundreds of blank

CD's that are just siting there. I would also laser engrave the logo or make the printout sticker for the CD and the cover. I used to do this for my closed clients before mp3 became the norm. On the off chance someone had a DVD player I would not be at a loss since these CD's will probably end up in the trash soon.

Phase two will be to take out a map of the immediate area and pinpoint the homes that have close friends and family. I would go to a sign shop or Home Depot and buy wooden stake signs and print yard sign for each of those individuals and have the bar code on them with simple instructions on the sign. Something like, "Order Girl Scout Cookies here" Just hold your camera phone to the little box and watch the magic cookie appear." I know that most do not understand how QR codes work. Maybe some of you do not even know what I am saying here. These are square images for marketing purposes like a digital fingerprint. They even look kind of like a fingerprint in a black and white random pattern. When you hold your camera up to the square, it will open a website automatically. Once a big fad in the marketing world, it never really caught on. But for the Scouts this may be a novelty and in the front yard as people walk their dogs with their smart phones, as a clever call to action might land a sale or two. I know I can purchase them online but I would add something like same day delivery for online orders. If Amazon can do it global, I am sure my wife can do this in the neighborhood. I'm a dead man for that comment.

Now after we have exhausted the typical delivery of the sign-up sheets at all the local businesses that we frequent. Assuming we got there first, I would take it to the streets. We would have a decorated wagon and each member of the team must be in uniform. The stealth drop for sure and as for the Columbo close this may not even be necessary. We will close. Here is the script and dialog that all Girl Scouts must use.

Walk up to the door and ring the bell and knock.

Hi my name is Scout with the Girls Scouts and it cookie season. We were just hoping you would be willing to buy some cookies this year, do you have a favorite?

Resident: Yes, Thin Mints.

Scout: Those are my favorite too. Most people buy 4 boxes, would you like more than 4?

Yes: Great, thanks for supporting us.

No: OK, then just one?

None: Oh did you already buy some?

No: We just don't want any?

Scout: That's OK. If you change your mind, Here is a flier for online orders and I would love it if you might share the link online. That would totally help us out this year.

Resident: No, we already bought some.

Scout: What kind did you buy? Thin mints?

Scout: How many did you buy?

Scout: I know that most of the thin mints make it about 20 minutes before they are gone in my house. Did you eat them all?

Resident: (Laughs and probably says yes or no)

Scout: perhaps I could interest you in replacing that one that went too fast. I have one thin mint with your name on it. But if you have not tried the new cookie, I would recommend that one. Who knows, it may be your new favorite. Please say yes. (Smile)

Resident: No

Scout: That's OK. If you change your mind, Here is a flier for online orders and I would love it if you might share the link online. That would totally help us out this year. Have a great day.

Smile and Skip away. I think skipping away would make anyone feel terrible about not supporting such a lovely child and this might get a sale or two extra when their heart melts.

I know there will be several other objections similar to any sales field.

Resident: The decision maker is not home.

Scout: A box of thin mints is only five dollars. I am sure your love of this cookie has already made the decision. Can you buy one box? (This is bold and should be used only with the cutest of smiles)

128

Resident: I do not have any cash.

Scout: Luckily for you we are now able to do the order on our smart phone, I can text you the link, what's your cell phone?

(Then don't look at the customer, look at your phone and recite the first three likely numbers of their area code with assumption and they will fill in the blank)

Resident: I am a diabetic.

Scout: I am sorry to hear that, my close friend is type one and it must be hard. Although we have a gluten-free option, this might not be the one for you. Hmm. (Physically pause and think with even a scratch of the head.) Well, how about showing someone you love or appreciate that you were thinking of them. Valentines is right around the corner too, so perhaps The Thanks-A-Lot shortbread cookies would be a great gift. They are only five dollars and you could still help us out.

Resident: I have a gluten allergy.

Scout: Then you are in luck. I ordered and brought along the new Caramel Chocolate chip and its gluten-free too! I really can't tell that the gluten is missing. But I am not sure what gluten even tastes like. (say this with a comical cutie style and you will melt the cookies and their heart into buying a box or four.)

I am finding out this year first hand how the world of the Girl Scout Cookies system works. I can't wait to see how my kid does. To those parents who have a little scout, good luck. Oh, and don't be eating all their cookies, they are supposed to be selling them.

Chapter Seven
Final Thoughts

I can say so much about what to do once you leave the engagement. In this chapter I will cover the three outcomes of the conversation at the door. These outcomes are also lined up with my theory of the three objectives at the door. Lead identification, Motivation identification and follow-up methods adjusted to motivation. The most common one is a "no" or what I would call a "cold" prospect. This is someone who gave you no sign of ever doing business such as you are in. Depending on your industry, you will create campaigns of follow up such as a real estate agent or insurance agents would do. This would build a slow relationship with the community and build brand awareness so that if they require your services, you might be top of mind. This is very costly for both time and money. Also, assuming that they are in fact not interested at all, you would not want to persist with communications too often and upset the resident. You can implement direct mail campaigns also, with a frequency that matches your budget. I know that in real estate you must commit to sending your marketing material by mail at least once a month for a year, then every other month forever. This would also include a flag on the lawn for the 4th of July and a Season's Greetings card in the winter.

The second level of motivated individual would be "maybe" or what I would label as a "warm" lead. No longer a suspect, but in fact this person showed that they might be interested. If the conversation went well, you got their information. If the conversation went not as planned, but you left there feeling like there was something else left to do then you must build a campaign for them too.

The lesser of the two would be an "lukewarm" lead that said maybe but was reluctant to give any information. Instead, they only took your card, or perhaps they said they have someone else in mind. If they are reluctant, it is still of the utmost importance that you complete the second objective of the three I teach. First is to identify if this is a lead? Maybe in this case. Second objective, when will they act/move/buy? This lukewarm individual who claims to have someone in mind but cannot say when is not that motivated and might warrant a letter or two along with light follow up. The difference between motivation and not motivated lies in the answer to question number two. "Do you think maybe later down the road you might reconsider, like (season)?"

If they give no information, you must take the address back to your CRM and build a complete contact from an online phone book or list providers. From there follow up is a delicate process since they did not give you their information. Saying I am the person who was there and they know you were not given that info might backfire. My approach is to just cold call them, assuming they are not on the do not call list. As for finding their email and sending them something that is something I avoid. I would try to sneak back in their graces by using the same approach I use at the door as I would on the phone. There is a high probability they do not know you are the one from the door. This is fine because they might be easier to connect with by phone. Once they are more receptive, I would do a Columbo like, *"you know what? We met a few weeks ago at the door, anyhow I would like to email you information…"* This is a matter of reengaging on different platforms that works best to elevate the relationship. In the individual's case saying they have someone else in mind, half the time this is a smoke screen and the mention of that person never comes up again. A pro tip here is that if they say a name and even mention a relationship like a relative of a friend from church or school, you might be out of luck. You can only ask that they interview more than one person. If they are open to this, then that relationship might not be that strong.

Taking this to the next half note is the actual "warm" that has in fact given you their information but they are anywhere from 3 months to three years away from moving. Yes, three years is still a warm lead. Especially if you are the first one in the door and you will be in the business in three years, you will be glad you followed up. If they are years away, I implement a follow-up campaign that begins with a thank-you card and I email them information on the values in the area. This pattern of letter, email and phone call to keep in touch is spread out over time depending on their motivation. If they are in three months, the frequency might me higher and if they are years, it will be less frequent. These "touches" begin with a higher frequency to solidify our relationship and brand awareness and then dissipate. I try not to bother them to avoid them unsubscribing from my email, tell me back off on the phone, or waste my money on stamps and paper. I am often moving these frequency plans from slow to fast depending on subsequent follow up and conversation. Sometimes these people change their mind and sometimes they move up their urgency. Sometimes they never answer their phone again and yet open my emails all the time. Read my chapter on the 5 Levels of Marketing to understand the varieties of follow up you can use to be at the right place at the right time.

The last and the best of these outcomes at the "yes" or "unicorn" door. This is that one in 4,000 for me. That one who says "yes." Well, they hardly ever say the actual word "yes", but it might as well be. The conversation goes well and they are open to hearing your pitch. If you cannot set an appointment to come back for a meeting, I recommend you stop what you are doing and get back to the office and prepare a full package of your services and get back to the door and deliver this in their hands. When you get back to the door, you cannot be attached to the outcome and expect anything more than just to impress them with your work ethic and readiness to provide value. Here is a sample return script. *"Mr. Owner, Sorry to bother you again but I wanted to leave you some information on the values in the area along with some services I provide.* (Stick it in their hands)*Please call me when you are ready. Thank you and have a nice day."* Sometimes you will be invited inside. Again, you can be ready to present and have contracts on the ready in your car. Sometimes they will say thanks, maybe even a "wow." Either way, if they do not receive you with a gesture to stay then leave. Follow up frequently but not too much. Following up with the individual is a delicate balance between going too hard and getting off their list and going too soft and having someone else take charge and get the contract.

There is no way to know just how much or how little to follow up. I say I would rather be told to "buzz off" than be told "thank you but we signed with the competition." It is an unfortunate part of our sales industry to be "that person", but for those of us who have lost one to a lack of follow up we know our options. I once had a guy, the four thousandth door I know for sure. It was a very hot lead who would sign a contract within 7 days for sure. I was walking up to the door, and he was walking out. I used all my methods taught in this book and it ended up with him saying in 2 weeks. I immediately went back to the office and created the package. I went back to the door, and he was not home. I left the package and called later that day. He said great and thank you. He also said to call him in two weeks. Knowing that an agent would approach him either online or in a circle of friends, whatever, I called him 7 days later. Then this happened. He said, "James, I told you to call me in two weeks, I just had my foot amputated this morning and I am not interested in you calling me again. I will not be using you to sell my house, lose my number." He hung up. Yeah, that happened. How was I to know? Had he said he was having surgery I would not have called for 2 weeks. I immediately sent a hand-written letter and even a video email with an apology. I never heard back from him. He listed 2 months later. It sold for less than what I could have gotten him. Oh well.

Tracking your efforts and knowing your numbers is critical to maintaining a realistic expectation. I know that every 100 doors I knock on, an average of 25 will open. Of those 25 contacts I will have one conversation with an individual who is considering selling. If I take 3 hours to knock on 100 doors and I speak to 25 people, I will always end the day with 1-3 names and numbers of homeowners who may be thinking of moving. If you repeat this five days a week, you could realistically generate 10 legitimate leads to fill your pipeline in one week.

In closing, I can offer this very important warning. Lead generation is very addictive. Once you find that door knocking works so well in getting leads, you will also fall into a trap of wanting to go back out and look for more. Trust me on this, I see it all the time; I am guilty of this. You will find that your follow up will suffer as it is put on a back burner. Knocking on that 100 or 200 doors feels productive. I get it, follow up is slow and painful. It is repetitious boredom with very little reward or rush. Having a great conversation is farther in between. I am referring to the telephone. The telephone is much faster at follow up than going back to the door. Especially if the results are about 25% of people are home and you have 100 leads in a follow up list meant to reach out today, and no one answers because only 6% of phones pick up. Going to the door may be even longer in time wasted only to find that they are not yet interested or that they are not home. I recommend that you try to reach them by phone first, but if they do not answer and you know that the time for them to act/buy/sell is yesterday, you must get to the door. Just do not under any circumstance go back out to hit the doors when you have a list of people to call back. You spend so much time generating these leads and you have such a good chance of closing for an appointment if only they would answer the phone. Exhaust all the 5 methods/levels of marketing and follow up to do what I call a blitz attack of follow-up until you get your answer. Whether that answer is not anymore, not yet, or next week you must keep rising that lead to the top of the priority or and the bottom of the funnel. You must get hundreds of these in my business to expect to pop one or two off a month. Do not get attached to the outcome of these and do not stop searching for new leads every day.

Get back to work! - Me

James Festini has been writing since his mid-teens when he began writing poetry and philosophy into a journal given to him by his mother. He continued writing, starting a series of collections that he would add to faithfully for the next 30-plus years. These journals contain some insights that are incorporated into his books. He draws on his own life experiences and lesson, learned to help others who may need to find their path in business and in life.

In his content, he shares how he and others weathered the Great Recession of 2008. Having suffered a devastating series of family events in 2011, he turned them into a helpful inspiration for others rather than succumb to depression. Like many, he lost everything. But unlike many, he worked hard to rebound quickly, and just a year later began incorporating old fashioned hustle and grit into his business, well ahead of others in his field. His goal is to enrich the lives of others.

James and his wife Nicole have called Southern California "home" for over 40 years, and have 4 wonderful children. He is also an avid wannabe tri-athlete and has completed 7 marathons. If he not full of it or does not get injured, he had better do an IronMan by 50 years of age.